# Higher Self Yoga:

# A Practical Teaching

# Higher Self Yoga:
# A Practical Teaching

## Nanette V. Hucknall

*Inner Journey Publishing*

Published by Inner Journey Publishing,
a division of
Higher Self Yoga, Inc.

ISBN: 978-1-7370162-1-2

Library of Congress Control Number: 2021942634

Cover Art: *"Comfort"* by Eleanor Goud, EleanorGoud.com

Dedicated to RHH, my spiritual teacher, and
My Mahatma, MM, who inspired this book and the
creation of the Higher Self Yoga teaching.

Their love and guidance made this possible.

# Acknowledgements

First, I want to thank our wonderful editor, Sharron Dorr, for her excellent work. I also wish to thank, Laraine Lippe, and Kathleen Frome, for doing the final review of the book. Additional thanks to our media people, Georgia Pettit and Hannah Stember, for their promotion of this book.

The main person who has my gratitude is Kathy Crowe, the Co-President of Inner Journey Publishing. She edited, designed the book, and made the changes that were needed, keeping everything in order and coordinating all the work of the others. She has been more than instrumental in making this book become a reality.

I also want to acknowledge the other Co-President of Inner Journey Publishing, Laraine Lippe, who handled the finances and much more that were needed to publish this book.

And thanks to the wonderful artist Eleanor Goud for the use of her painting on the cover of this book and other Higher Self Yoga materials.

# Table of Contents

# Introduction

When you start to work with a spiritual teaching, you will find obstacles and challenges that can often keep you from moving forward. This book addresses some of the situations that usually happen on the spiritual path.

In working with the Higher Self you will discover that it is not only the part within you that is seeking God Consciousness, but it is also the part in you that can help you in practical ways to heal inner wounds and move through those challenges that you will meet along the way.

When people become interested in a yoga teaching, some will feel very enthusiastic and want to become fully involved. Others will be more cautious and explore several teachings to determine the one that feels right to them. In both cases, it's important to decide if you are ready to begin this quest.

Your Higher Self understands you and knows when you are ready to explore the spiritual path. It is your guiding light on the way, whether you choose Higher Self Yoga or any other spiritual teaching.

In all yoga teachings there are spiritual teachers, or what in the east are called gurus. These teachers are advanced yogis who have studied their teachings for many years and have achieved what are called higher initiations. Their purpose, which is part of any yoga teaching, is to guide and help those students achieve what they themselves have accomplished.

If you have chosen to become a disciple of one of these teachers, then you have committed yourself to the spiritual journey. You can also choose just to study the esoteric or spiritual part of a teaching without becoming a disciple; you can remain a student who wants to learn, but doesn't want to commit her/himself to a teacher in striving for what is called God Consciousness. The Sanskrit word yoga means "union with God," or what we call the Source.

Doing the exercises in this book will help you determine whether you are ready to start this journey. It is not an easy one—it is full of challenges and obstacles. The psychological work is very much a major part of this teaching as we believe that psychological problems will stop someone from growing spiritually. The classes and books of Higher Self Yoga emphasize psychology, and help people to see and overcome their negative traits, and also to become more aware of their positive ones. Self-awareness is important for every yogi; only when someone truly understands her/himself can that person go through a transformation and achieve spiritual growth.

The yoga journey is very individual. It is a process that winds its way through jungles, full of darkness and hidden desires, and up mountains that reach heights revealing worlds that are unknown and inspirational. When you are ready the path is there.

Rather than say he or she throughout the book, in odd-number chapters I use he and in even-number chapters I use she, but of course the material applies to both genders.

It is recommended that you do the Higher Self Exercises described at the end of this book, so you can develop a feel for what it is to be in touch with your Higher Self as you do the exercises.

### Chapter One

## Using your Higher Self When You Have a Problem to Overcome

Many people will react in an emotional manner when they are confronted with a difficult problem. They often make decisions that are spontaneous and not thought out. Basically, these types of people blame their mistakes on others and feel they are victims as a result.

Without a doubt, these people can make a hard situation even worse than it has to be. The following is an example of what I am saying.

Many years ago, in a small village in southern France, lived Edmond and Cerise, who were siblings in a large family of farmers. When they became adults, neither of them married, so they ended up living together and taking care of a small farm that their parents had left them. All the others in their family had married and moved to cities or towns that were much larger. In those days, communication was limited, making family news almost impossible to come by.

One day when Cerise was feeding the chickens, she heard a shot fired close to the home. She ran to where the sound had come from and discovered Edmond unconscious, lying on the ground with a shotgun in his hand. Something had gone wrong, and the gun had backfired, causing Edmond to be wounded in his upper arm. Cerise screamed and went running back and forth, not knowing what to do. She thought Edmond must be dead but in her panic never checked his pulse or looked at the wound, which was bleeding profusely. Instead, she saddled a horse and rode to town to get help. It took her a half an hour to get there, find the doctor, and ride back.

By then Edmond was in serious condition because of his loss of blood. Also, the wound was covered with dirt and should have been cleaned right away. By the time the doctor arrived, infection had taken over. It took weeks for Edmond to recover, and his arm had to be amputated.

His friends all realized that Cerise had caused Edmond to become an invalid because of her lack of knowing what to do. They all blamed her, and later on, Edmond felt the same way. It made Cerise angry and bitter that she was being blamed for what she thought was Edmond's carelessness.

They continued to live together. Cerise had to do most of the farm work and hire outside help for the heavier tasks. Before they had been good, loving siblings, sharing a life that was fairly comfortable. After the accident, they became hateful and mean to each other, living an unhappy life until they died.

If you are in a situation in which something serious suddenly happens, it would be good to take a couple of breaths, link with your heart, and try to use your heart to guide you as to what would be the best thing to do.

Often it might seem that there isn't time to do this, particularly if the situation is critical. But if Cerise had calmed herself and immediately checked to see if Edmond was alive, then she could have taken a minute to assess what needed to be done. It was obvious that it was his arm was that was injured, and it was bleeding.

Her intuition would have told her to apply a tourniquet on the arm to help stop the bleeding; and, seeing the dirt, she would have gotten some water to wash it off. She would have also tried to bring him back to consciousness before she left, so that he wouldn't wake up to find himself alone in the dirt. All these steps required rational thinking, but to have that, she needed first to calm down. Taking some deep breaths and linking with her heart would have helped her do that right away.

There are other situations that happen in life, of course, that aren't as critical as this one. Those situations can give a person more time to resolve them.

A person would like to think that when something happens, he would always be able to take the right action. This is often not true, though, mainly because significant situations can cause a variety of emotions, and, when that happens, emotions cloud the right decisions.

For example, your wife is having a child and goes into labor. You are responsible for getting her to the hospital right away. Maybe you are prepared to follow a routine to do so in a calm manner. This preparation makes you feel confident. It's just about doing what had been planned.

But maybe the baby is coming too fast, and the wife's water has broken. Driving her to the hospital would be nerve-racking—if the baby comes in the car, you would have to find a place to stop to help your wife. That situation wasn't thought about or planned. Staying at home for the delivery also wasn't planned. What to do? If you linked with your heart and Higher Self, when your wife went into labor you would call a taxi or a neighbor to take you to the hospital so that you could be in the back with her. Or, if the baby were coming too soon, then you would call some women neighbors to come to the house to help; and, while you are waiting for them, you would make your wife comfortable and get the things that might be needed.

Again, this is a situation calling for sudden decisions, but it allows a little more time to become calm and link with the Higher Self than dealing with a gunshot wound does. Most situations that need resolution usually provide a lot more time to resolve them. Having more time can be good and sometimes not so good. The not-so-good happens when a situation is thought about too much. Resolving something could be easy, but often people become so involved in the problem that they spoil the outcome, not only by overthinking the situation but also by getting more involved emotionally. What could be a simple answer becomes confusing and challenging, making a satisfactory resolution difficult.

Why does this happen? There are lots of reasons. Some of the reasons you have might be the following:

1. The situation involves a couple of people you love, and you have to not take sides in any way. You feel what you have learned is accurate.
2. The resolution will cause some problems for you or your family.
3. You feel stuck because if you do the right thing, it will make your work more difficult.
4. Your work ethic can cause you to make a wrong decision, even when you know what the best outcome should be.
5. Your life can become complicated if you do what you feel is right.
6. Without a doubt, if the situation isn't properly resolved, you feel you will be considered a failure.
7. Your livelihood is dependent on the right resolution.

8.  Your children can be affected by what you do if it is wrong.
9.  Your spouse will be angry at you if you do what you know is correct.
10. Sometimes, you're not certain that you are capable of doing the correct thing.
11. When challenged, you feel upset and can't think clearly.
12. You fear your friends will leave you if you make a mistake.
13. This decision could take your life in a direction that is unknown and scary to you.
14. What if you make the wrong decision?
15. What will happen to you if you make a mistake?

These are just a few of the issues that stop a person from resolving something that normally could be easy to resolve.

*Exercise One:*

*Think back through the year and write down any problems that you had to resolve. Then prioritize them, putting the most difficult one first and the least difficult one last.*

*Then, taking one at a time starting with the top one, ask your Higher Self the following questions:*

1.  *When I first had this problem, what was my main feeling?*
2.  *Was it easy for me to come to decide what I needed to do?*
    - *If the answer is no, ask: What was the difficulty I encountered?*
3.  *Ask: Did I have any emotion around this difficulty?*

- *If the answer is yes, ask: Why?*
4. *Did I handle this emotion quickly, or did I get immersed in it?*
   - *If the answer is yes, ask: Why?*
5. *Was I able to overcome this difficulty?*
   - *If the answer is no, ask: Why?*
6. *Do I feel I made the right decision concerning this problem?*
   - *If the answer is no, ask: Why?*
7. *When I look back at this problem, could I have done something else that would have been better?*
   - *If the answer is yes, ask: What would have been a better solution?*
8. *What did I need to learn from this experience?*
   - *Regarding your answer to that question, ask: Did I do that?*
   - *If the answer is no, ask: Why not? What am I not learning, and how can I learn it?*
9. *Is this situation something that has happened to me before?*
   - *If the answer is yes, ask: What was the outcome? Was it the same, better, or worse than what has happened now?*
10. *If the situation has happened before, ask: Have I learned from being in this situation before what I needed to learn to handle it better now?*
    - *If the answer is no, ask: Why not? What am I not learning, and how can I learn it?*

Next, it's important to consider the problem you had and look more carefully at your feelings when you were going through it.

*Exercise Two:*

*Regarding the problem you are working with, look at the list of fifteen issues on page 4. Go over each one and ask yourself: Did I feel like this at all when I had this problem? If the answer is yes to one or even several of the issues, then ask your Higher Self the following questions:*

1. *At the time, was I aware that I was feeling like this?*
   - *If the answer is no, ask: Why not?*
   - *If the answer is yes, ask: Did I do anything with that feeling?*
2. *Did that feeling affect my decision-making?*
   - *If the answer is yes, ask: How did it affect it?*
3. *Take that answer and ask: Can I now look at this issue and learn from it?*
   - *If the answer is yes, ask: What is the best way for me to do that?*

Often the same problem happens over and over again, mainly because the person hasn't learned what he or she needed to learn. It's always important to ask yourself why the same thing happens to you so many times. Then work with your Higher Self to help you understand the cause of the problem and what it is you need to learn so that it won't happen again. The following story illustrates this issue:

Evan, a man in his mid-thirties, wanted to marry Jennifer, who was the same age. They had been together for five years and even lived together for three of those years, but every time Evan asked Jennifer to marry him, she would make excuses. She loved him but didn't want to get engaged or married.

Evan wanted to be married and have children, but Jennifer was very worried that, if she married at all, she would be unfaithful. When she was younger, she had several affairs and was usually the person who broke up the relationship. She had fallen in love with and become engaged to two of those previous men. But then, almost right away, she met someone else and had an affair. Both the fiancés had found out eventually and left her.

Each time this happened, Jennifer was very upset and felt very guilty. When she thought about what she had done, she really couldn't understand her actions. The only thing she could think of was that her parents had a bad, unhappy marriage, and she was afraid the same thing could happen to her. So, she decided it was best not to marry.

She was afraid to tell Evan her fears because then he also might leave her. She even agreed to have a child and said that maybe they could get married after that. He couldn't understand what the problem was and asked her to do therapy to find out what she was afraid of.

She didn't want to do that, either, but she felt she had to; otherwise, Evan might then leave her anyway. When she told her therapist her story, he asked her more about her previous affairs and why she was the one always to break up. She said she had really cared about each of the men but always found something in the relationship that didn't work for her. Exploring those things in therapy proved that they were very minor reasons.

Her response to that insight was that obviously she had never wanted to get married. She thought perhaps she could not get married and hoped that Evan would still want to live with her and have children.

When he questioned her about their relationship, it seemed that even the things she didn't like about Evan didn't bother her like they did some of the others she had affairs with did. When they explored the relationship with the men she was engaged to, she saw she had accepted them in the same way she did Evan and that began to confuse her more. Why, if she loved them, and she agreed to marry them, did she jump in bed with someone else? Maybe she was just innately promiscuous.

Her father and mother had fought a lot and had opposite personalities. Not much love there, but she felt they had still been faithful to each other. It seemed that all her relationships were the complete opposite to her parent's marriage.

Her therapist decided to do some inner-child work with Jennifer to see if what she remembered was correct. When she did a regression to the age of three, she saw that her parents really had loved each other; they were very affectionate and loving to each other and to her.

Then when she was five something happened that changed everything. It took a while to see it all. It started one day when she and her mother were going for a walk in a nearby park. A man approached them and greeted her mother by throwing his arms around her—kissing her on the lips. Her mother was surprised but responded to him warmly. She then introduced him to Jennifer, saying he was an old college friend she hadn't seen for many years. His name was Charles, and he knelt down and shook Jennifer's hand. They walked into the playground; and, while Jennifer played with some of the other children, her mother and Charles sat on a bench talking.

When Jennifer looked over once in a while, she was surprised to see her mother clasping Charles's hands and both of them looking intensely at each other. Later Charles took them to a restaurant for lunch, and again Jennifer felt their intense feelings for each other. When they went home later in the afternoon, Jennifer's mother asked her not to mention Charlie to her father. She explained that

Charles was an old friend of hers, but her father didn't know him and might feel left out.

For the next few days, Charles would meet them at the playground. One day her mother asked a friend there if she would watch Jennifer while she and Charles went shopping. This happened a couple of times. One day Charles didn't come, and when Jennifer asked about him, her mother said he had to go back to where he lived. He had come here on business and that was now over. Her mother seemed sad and reminded Jennifer not to say anything to her father. That evening Jennifer was playing with a new doll, and her father asked her if her mother had bought it for her. Without thinking, she said, no, Charles had when he and Mummy went shopping. He asked who Charles was and she said, "Oh, I'm sorry, I wasn't supposed to say anything."

Her father got furious and left to find her mother. She could hear them yelling at each other. Jennifer was scared and very upset because she had said something. When she saw her mother again in tears, her mother screamed at her, "Why did you do that? I told you never to tell your father about Charles."

From then on, the relationship between Jennifer's parents had been the way she always remembered it. They fought over everything, and it seemed that the main reason they stayed together was because of Jennifer. Finally, when Jennifer went to college they got divorced.

Jennifer never remembered what happened with Charles and her mother, but unconsciously she always blamed herself for ruining her parents' marriage, so she felt she didn't deserve ever to have a happy marriage herself. Part of her self-punishment was to be unfaithful to any man she loved so that he would break up with her. Even though she had been faithful to Evan for five years, a part of her still believed she would ruin the relationship if she married him. She was afraid she would repeat what her mother had done to her father and that would be her final punishment.

After a year of intense therapy, healing her inner child's fears, Jennifer could accept Evan's proposal and feel joy in knowing marriage with him would be happy and fulfilling.

This story illustrates how negative patterns can control someone unconsciously. If Jennifer had married Evan without doing the work in therapy, she probably would have again punished herself by having an affair with someone else—also making certain that Evan would find out.

Often someone follows inner feelings that come from things that have happened to them in their childhood.

*Exercise Three:*

*Again, take the top problem on the list that you are working with and ask your Higher Self the following questions:*

1. *Is there something in this problematic situation that in any way relates to something that happened in my childhood?*
   - *If the answer is yes, ask: What happened?*
     - *About that happening, ask: How was it resolved?*
     - *If it was never resolved, ask: How did the situation affect me?*
     - *If it was resolved, also ask: How did the situation affect me?*
       - *If the answer is yes, ask: Did I do anything with that feeling?*
2. *Has this childhood situation in any way affected the way in which I resolved the problem that I am working with now?*

- *If it has affected it, ask: If this situation hadn't happened to me in my childhood, would I have resolved the current problem differently?*
- *If the answer is yes, ask: How would I have resolved it*

After you have worked with the problem you chose to work with, it would be good to look back at your life and choose something that happened to you that was extremely important—something that might have changed what you did in the following years. It should be something that affected you and at the time was a problem for you to resolve.

Do all the above exercises for this situation as you did with the last problem.

Realize that working with the Higher Self is very important to do when you are confronted with a decision or a problem that needs to be resolved. The Higher Self always knows what is in your unconscious that can direct you to do something. If that direction has emotions attached, they can influence you into making wrong decisions. Therefore, it's important always to check with your Higher Self about any resolution you make to be certain it is the right one.

**Chapter Two**

## The Higher Self Can Help Your Relationships

Many people feel the Higher Self is meant to be used only spiritually, as it is the part in you that contains your higher characteristics and can also help you come closer to whatever spiritual belief you have. This much is certainly true, but the Higher Self also has a strong practical side to its nature. Its main purpose is to help you grow spiritually, but it also wants to help you overcome any problems you may encounter in your daily life.

Obviously, if you are in a negative relationship with someone, that will affect you spiritually as well as make you prone to attracting negative energy around you. This can cause you to become negative yourself, which will affect your actions and can cause you to have negative karma as a consequence.

Let's look at what can happen if you are in an adverse relationship that causes you to attract negative energy to the place where you live or work.

First, you can lose your connection to your Higher Self, placing you in a position where you don't have the positive resources that it can provide you. Then, you might make mistakes that will hurt you in your personal life and also in your work life. The following is a story that illustrates what could happen.

Many years ago, in a small town in northern Scotland, there lived a family of fishermen. There were the parents, Bonnie and Donald, and their two children, Craig and Keith, along with Arabella, Bonnie's cousin.

After her husband had died, Arabella was alone in the world. She had no children who could take care of her. Bonnie heard about Arabella's predicament and, after a family conference, invited her to live with them. Their cottage was fairly large, so there was an extra room.

Arabella had previously lived in a town that was more cosmopolitan than the town that Bonnie lived in, a small fishing village on the coast. Craig and Keith, then fifteen and twelve, were already helping their father in his fishing boat, so Bonnie and Arabella were left to themselves most of the day. Both women spent time doing various household chores. Bonnie was a good baker, and cook, and spent a lot of her time preparing food for all of them to eat. Arabella turned out to be good at sewing and making clothing, especially for the boys. So, it looked like she was a good addition to the family.

After a month of being there, Arabella, having met some of the other women in the village, suggested that they have a weekly sewing club. Although Bonnie had no desire to attend, she said it was fine with her to have the meetings in their house. The women could meet in the living room, which was separate from the kitchen where Bonnie spent most of her time.

Unbeknown to her, Arabella was a huge gossip, and started to make up stories about Bonnie's and Donald's marriage. These stories were personal in content and very exaggerated. Soon rumors were moving around the village about how difficult Bonnie was and how she bossed Donald all the time. The boys also were included in the gossip as being controlled by Bonnie.

Bonnie was totally unaware of any of this, but she did notice that, when she met someone in the village, they were no longer as friendly as they used to be. She sometimes took cookies to a few of these people whom she had known for most of her life, but some now said they weren't eating sweets anymore. What Bonnie didn't know was that not only was Arabella disparaging her to her friends, but she was also telling them that Bonnie said negative things about them.

Every week, Donald went to the village pub to drink and play darts with his friends. Some men he was close to asked if things were okay with Bonnie, that their wives were telling them things that sounded strange and offensive about Bonnie's relationship with him and the boys. They also said that Bonnie was telling Arabella negative things about the women themselves, and they didn't want to have anything more to do with her.

Donald was very surprised; it was difficult for him to believe that Bonnie could be like that. That night when they were alone, he told her what his friends had said and added, "They told me that you even talked about me negatively. I know that can't be true. Where are these rumors coming from?"

"Of course they are not true, I never did that. How can they be saying that about me?" And Bonnie broke into tears.

"I'm sorry. When I defend you, they obviously believe I am lying about it."

Bonnie thought for a minute. "It must be coming from somewhere. I have been noticing strange behavior from my friends, almost like I am an outcast."

"OK, I will talk to Brice to find out what has been happening. I think he would be honest with me."

When Donald conferred with Brice, one of his pub friends, Brice told him that the men's wives had heard this news in their sewing circle; it was Arabella who was expressing her concern for Donald and his sons.

Since Arabella was living with Donald and Bonnie, everyone believed her. Why would she lie about it? After all, the couple had helped her and taken her into their home. When Arabella spoke, she always expressed her gratitude and said she felt bad to see these things happening in the family.

Donald was furious. When he told Brice it was all lies, Brice looked as if he didn't believe him, even saying, "I find it strange that Arabella would lie about Bonnie, since Bonnie has been her benefactor."

When Donald told Bonnie, she also became very angry. "How dare she say those things about me. We have taken her in and given her a nice home to live in, and this is the way she repays us! I think we need to confront her and find out why she did this and make her tell our friends the truth."

"But if we do that," said Donald. "Everyone will think we are abusive. That would make things even worse."

Bonnie started crying again, "She's ruined our lives here."

"I think we need to talk to Magnus," said Donald. "He may know what to do." The next day they went to see Magnus (who was their minister) and told him the whole story. Magnus was thoughtful for some time. He walked back and forth in the room and finally sat down and looked at them.

"This is a good example of manipulation," he said. "Arabella obviously wants to get rid of you, Bonnie; maybe she wants Donald to divorce you and marry her."

"Oh my God! What can we do?" Bonnie exclaimed.

"It's important that you confront her, but not by herself," Magnus said.

"You also need to confront all the women in the sewing group whom you have known for years. Did any of them talk to you about what Arabella was saying?"

"No, they never did, they just started becoming more distant," Bonnie answered.

"Well, I feel it is very hurtful that none of them told you about it. You need to confront not just Arabella but all of them." Magnus then reassured Bonnie that doing this would put all the facts on the table. If these women still believed Arabella, then they were not people she wanted to have as friends.

"This is going to be very hard for me to do," said Bonnie. "I've known these women for years."

Donald added, "I will be there with you to help you."

Magnus said, "No, Bonnie, this is something you need to do alone. I will give you an exercise to do beforehand. It will give you the courage and help you say the right things." Then he told them about the Higher Self, and how to connect to it.

The next time the sewing circle met, Bonnie came into the room and said she needed to talk to all of them.

Looking at Arabella, she told her she now knew Arabella had been slandering her to all her friends, saying things that were out and out lies about her. Looking at Aileen, she said, "Aileen, Brice told Donald that you and the others here believe these lies."

Pausing, she looked at each woman and said, "I have been your friend for many years. Ella, you and I went to school together and have been friends since that time. Olivia, you and I always run a booth at our yearly festivals. Jessica, how many times did we bake cakes for the church? After all those years of doing projects together, you all would certainly know by now if I were controlling or bossy."

The group started glancing at each other. "Yet, you believed Arabella and not one of you came to me and told me what she was saying. Instead you all started to believe her. This is a huge disappointment to me."

She turned to Arabella, "I have given you a home and safe place to live, and have helped and supported you after your loss, and you have repaid me and my family by spreading vicious lies about me. You even told people untruths about my relationship with Donald,. but fortunately, he knows the kind of person I am, and when he heard these lies, he was very angry."

As the women left, each one apologized to Bonnie. When they were all gone, Bonnie told Arabella to pack her things, that Donald would take her anywhere she wanted to go. Maybe there was a friend or another member of the family she could live with.

When they saw Magnus again, they thanked him for his help, and Bonnie said she felt very clear and focused and strong because of the Higher Self exercise he gave her.

If you are in a negative relationship with someone, it's important either to change it or, if that can't happen, to leave. Sometimes you may believe the relationship is fine and not be aware that the person is saying negative things about you. Such behavior is always harmful because those negative thoughts will literally reach you and make you feel tired or ill, especially if you have a close relationship with the person.

When fight and yell at each other, that also affects both people physically. It takes twenty-four hours for the chemistry in the body to go back to normal after someone is irritated. People living in such conditions can eventually come down with a serious illness. Conversely, living with someone you love and have a happy relationship with will bring positive energy and well-being.

Exercise One:
*Think about all your relationships, both good and bad. Include people that you have to work with. Make a list of the*

*ones that tend to be negative, then prioritize the list, putting the worst one on top. Take the top name, connect with your Higher Self and ask it the following questions:*

1. *How can I best deal with this person?*
2. *Is there any bad karma between us?*
   - *If the answer is yes, ask to know more about it.*
3. *When we have a negative interaction, how can I best change the energy?*
4. *If I can't change it, what is the best way for me to deal with it?*
5. *If I become negative, what is the best process for me to use to rid myself of this energy?*
6. *If I need to break up with this person, what is the best way for me to do this?*
7. *If I can't break up with this person, what is the best way for me to deal with this person so that the energy isn't negative?*
8. *How can I change my negative feelings toward this person?*

Obviously, if you work with someone you have a negative relationship with, it is best to try to remain neutral and not allow the person's negativity to affect you. Often the negative person is someone who is depressed and moody.

Constantly living or working with someone like that is difficult.

If it is someone you love, then it's best to try to persuade the person to seek help. If it is someone you work with, it's best to put a glass bell around yourself when you are with the person, otherwise the negative energy can affect you.

Negative energy can also cause you to feel emotional, and when that happens the emotions can make you vulnerable to the other person's feelings. This is how fights happen. To avoid any conflict, it's best to come up with a solution from your Higher Self, a solution that would best help you to remain calm.

*Exercise Two:*

*Ask your Higher Self: What would be the best way for me to stay calm in an emotional situation?*

There are many calming exercises, but remember, what is good for someone else may not work as well for you. That's why it's best to ask your Higher Self for an exercise to do.

Negative relationships usually come from negative past lives. It's always good to resolve the karma in the present life, so you no longer have to return with the person again. This is sometimes difficult to do, but the Higher Self can help you.

*Exercise Three:*

*Look through your list of negative relationships and highlight those people your Higher Self said you had karma with. Taking the top name and the answer your Higher Self told you concerning the karma, ask your Higher Self:*

1. *Is it possible for me to resolve this karma in this lifetime?*
   - *If the answer is yes, ask: What is the best way for me to do this?*
   - *If the answer is no, ask: Why can't I resolve it in this lifetime?*
2. *Take that answer and ask: Is there anything I can do that will lessen the karma?*

Sometimes the karma is very difficult to resolve, but there is always a way to lessen it, in case you have to return with the person. Always try to do this, but never let yourself become a victim in the situation. That only causes more karma to be made that has to eventually be worked out.

*Exercise Three:*

*Now look at the negative karma you have made with others in past lives. If that person is back with you, then the person may be directing negative feelings toward you.*

*Look at your list again and try to determine which relationship would have that configuration. Then check those results with your Higher Self to determine if you were correct in your valuation.*

*Take the Higher Self's answers and ask the Higher Self the following questions about the top person:*

1. *Can you tell me more about how I treated this person in a past life?*
   - *If the answer is no, ask: Why not?*
   - *If the answer is yes, ask for more information on how I treated this person in a past life.*
2. *Is it possible for me to eliminate this negative karma in this life?*
   - *If the answer is no, ask: Why not?*
3. *If the answer is yes, ask: What is the best way for me to do this?*

Sometimes karma can be eliminated by trying to send love to the person. But to do so, you must really feel that love in your heart, which is often difficult for a person to do. If you try to do this and find it too difficult, ask your Higher Self: How can I develop love for this person so I can heal this karma?

Remember that karma is often very subtle, and your lower nature will not want you to resolve it. Watch for any interference when you do this work. The best safeguard is to keep asking your Higher Self if there is interference and then ask for help to stop it from happening.

Negative energy can also be part of your community, your town, your state, and your country. When you are in a meeting, try to always be aware if someone is there who has negative energy and is causing the harmony to be disrupted. The only thing you can do then is to ask your Higher Self to help you send positive energy coming from your heart, around the room, or at any large gathering. Also, try not to get caught up in a mob situation that can occur in outside protests.

Do your best to send good energy around those people nearest you. Always try to be positive no matter what the situation. Stay calm and linked with your Higher Self in any difficult situation. It gives you the ability to know the proper action to take.

Relationships need to be positive; otherwise, you live a life that is stressful and harmful. Do your best to surround yourself with people you love and who love you. Take care of yourself in all your surroundings. That will help you move forward spiritually.

## Chapter Three
# Looking at Your Past in a New Way

When someone is older, he often looks back at his life and thinks either that he has done well or that he should have done better. This is true for most people and does not in any way relate to a person's upbringing. It is part of human nature for a person to judge his actions in the past and either to accept the mistakes he made or to feel he did the best he could at the time. But often the person judges himself and considers his past actions major mistakes that ruined his life.

For example, a young man decides to marry a schoolmate and immediately regrets having done so. In particular, if the marriage produces a child right away, it takes away any freedom the young man has. Regrets, regrets, regrets continue to cloud this person's existence. When that happens, then the person looks back and realizes that, if he had waited to get married, his life would have been 100 percent better. He would now be successful and have stability in his older years. Often, self-evaluation is full of such "why didn't I's?" that can only cause the person to feel like a failure.

If a young person looks back on his life, there may still be judgments, but because there is time to change things the person's outlook will be more positive. He can see better ways to act that will change his life and be fulfilling. It is also easier to learn from his mistakes and take that learning into the future so that he won't make the same mistakes again.

This is what reviewing the past should be like. Yet does it actually happen this way, or would it be an exception to the pattern the person has already put in place? That is an important question to ask oneself. Other questions to ask are: How can I change the way I look at my life? Is this possible?

It's important to look at your life in a way that is very different from what you have already stated. Ask yourself: Is it possible for me to stop judging myself and also judging others? How is it possible for me to look at my past with new eyes, without dwelling on the mistakes I have made, but seeing the positive and the lesson learned to be used now and in the future?

Seeing yourself means being honest, having clear insight, and being open to learning who you were in the past and who you are now. How often does a person accept the past even when it is full of emotional pain? How often does a person realize truths learned and know what was good versus what was wrong action? If someone works with his heart in evaluating his past, then he will know those truths and also feel that life has brought him something of value that he can hold and cherish.

Letting go of a painful past is one of the most difficult things a person can do. You would think it would be easy, but it never is. This is because people, as a whole, tend to hold on to negative events in their lives—never fully releasing them. If the person himself caused the action, he will hold on to it as a form of self-punishment. If it was an action someone else did to him, he will hold on to it because it excites his need to get even. Even if he doesn't act on that need, he will hold on to the need to do something in revenge. Holding on like this will only cause the person to live a life full of upset and self-defense.

How many people do you know who still hold grudges about something that happened to them twenty years ago? How many people still talk about making mistakes when they were younger and didn't have the good sense to know what to do about a situation they were in? How many people project the judgment they've made about those situations onto others, either hoping that the others will do better than they have or expecting similar bad results? The following is a story that illustrates this truth:

Evan and Lois were very much in love when they met in college and married right after they graduated. Evan then continued his education to become a lawyer, while Lois took on the burden of working while he went to school. During that time, they lived a frugal life, socializing very little and never going out because of their lack of funds. They kept some friends, but many fell away because of their lifestyle. Lois felt resentful about her life during this time, but she never complained as she was still very much in love with Evan.

After he graduated, Evan got a job with a law firm in Chicago, and Lois also found a job there as a manager's assistant in a corporation. Lois thought that then they would have more money to go out with friends again and live a fuller life. But that didn't happen because Evan's job entailed long hours during the week and some meetings on weekends. He was so busy he often didn't come home but stayed in Chicago overnight to avoid the long commute home.

They had been living in a town an hour and a half from the city. Lois suggested they move to suburbs closer to Chicago so that both their commutes would be shorter. Doing so would be much more expensive, though, and Evan was paying off student loans, so they stayed where they were.

After the loans were paid, they started to save money for a house. By then Evan was doing better financially but still had to work long hours. He told Lois that no one at his firm had normal hours—this was to be expected in his business. They could only hope to buy a house closer to the city; and, when he had time off, they could spend it having fun together. But such time off happened very infrequently.

Lois's career was also improving, and she got a job as a manager that brought them more income. She decided to go back to school and get her MBA to help her advance her career in business. When she graduated, she got a better job in a large corporation, and with the better income they finally bought a house nearer to the city in a very plush community.

Both were doing well but spent little time together except for some weekends and short vacations. They had wanted to have a family; and, since Lois was now in her thirties, they decided to start trying. Originally, Lois had wanted to be a stay-at-home mother. Now, they had enough money for her not to work, but she didn't want to give up her career, as it was blooming.

They agreed to hire a nanny for any children, and Lois gave birth to the perfect children to create the family they wanted—a boy and a girl.

Their careers took them more and more away from home and the children. By then they had a live-in nanny; and, since they both were working late and doing more traveling, the only time they had with the children was on weekends, which proved to be hectic and not well organized.

By this time, Evan and Lois had started quarreling over little things that went wrong. Finally, when the children were still young, they decided to separate and eventually got divorced. Evan bought a condo in town, and Lois kept the house, the children, and all that went with them. Even though Evan gave her a good allowance for all the costs, she felt it was she who had the burden of having to take care of everything.

The children were starting to have problems. They fought a lot and only wanted to be with the nanny. Evan rarely took them on the weekends; and, now that he was living in the city, he started to date and go out more. Lois was becoming more and more hostile to him and felt she had made a huge mistake in marrying him. At first in their lives together she had supported him; then she had gotten stuck in a place where she had no friends. And now, again, she was stuck in a place with the children and still no time for friends or a normal life. She knew Evan was dating and having a good time, and she felt like the loser. Depressed and irritated because of her feelings of failure and low self-worth, she frequently struck out at the children and no longer felt the love she had for them when they were younger.

After a couple of years of self-abasement, Lois was talked into going into therapy by a friend at work. Her therapist worked with Lois's feelings of lack of worth and helped her realize that her life wasn't over, that she could still find love, and that she needed to help her children, who were feeling sad and upset with what was happening in their home.

The thing that was hardest for Lois to do was to let go of her feelings of having made a huge mistake by marrying Evan. Her lost years were like a rope around her neck. She kept thinking: What if I hadn't married him? Where would I be now? What could I have had all these years? How stupid I was!

Looking at her past was dragging her down into a deep depression. When she finally dropped the thoughts and started building the future, her life changed. She got a new job that was very good and also gave her more time to be at home with her children. And she had time to see friends and enjoy her life as well. She was very attractive and soon had men asking her out. Even when she was attracted to someone, she was careful to not get involved with anyone like Evan, who was a workaholic and a loner. The men she was interested in were family-oriented and also wanted to spend time with her.

Lois eventually married a nice man who was a professional with a good job that didn't require long hours. Her children now had a stepfather with whom they grew close. Evan kept his single life, doing the same thing and rarely taking his children out. He felt he was fine and loved his lifestyle. Only when he was much older, alone with no family, did he look back at his life and wonder if maybe he had made mistakes. He ended up a partner in the firm with a lot of money and a lonely life.

It's important to look at your past in a way that is clearly discerning without any self-judgment. Learning from the past is very important, but let that learning be based on who you were at the time. See yourself only in terms of how much knowledge you had about life then and how much information you had about who you wanted to become. Judging yourself won't help you to understand who you truly are in terms not just of who you were then but also of who you are in total—including what characteristics you brought into this life and what karma you have had to pay off.

Often mistakes are caused by karma and the attraction it has that causes you not to see clearly. Relationships, especially with family members, are mostly karma, but karma can also make you react with others in ways you don't fully understand until you are no longer in the situation. Karma is a strong provoker that can make you do things that later you are ashamed of. You can avoid doing wrong actions to see how karma may be affecting your behavior.

When you look at the past, try to see how karma was a main influencer. Check your reactions and feel whether your karma was involved. If it wasn't, then check what happened and listen to your heart to discover what was motivating you at the time. Do the following exercises in a calm, centered, and focused manner. Try to avoid any judgments, and try to be open to all the ways you could have changed the outcome—ways that you didn't see at the time.

Take your time when you do these next exercises, realizing you can still learn and grow as an outcome.

*Exercise One:*

*Look at your life from the time you were a teenager up to the present time. Think about all the major things you went through, events that were difficult, soul rendering, and full of indecision and also caused you to do something that affected your life thereafter.*

*Write a paragraph about what happened, how it affected you, how it felt at the time, and how much it influenced you as you moved on.*

*The event could be something physical, psychological, and/or even spiritual. It could be something that caused problems in a relationship or even the destruction of the relationship. Or, it could be something extremely positive that resulted in you moving forward successfully. Remember, you are looking at the things that happened to you that were wonderful, exciting, and fulfilling, as well as those that were very difficult and even harmful.*

*Make two lists: one of events that were positive and one of events that were negative. Include on the lists only the events that have deeply affected your life.*

When you work with these lists, work with a negative occurrence and then a positive one. Don't look at more than four events total at a time, and always put a few days in between. After you finish the work on one group of four, look at the next four you will be working with, because on the days in between, more feelings may arise that are connected to them.

You may ask what the purpose is in reliving these things, especially when they are sad and hurtful. Looking at them again can change your perspective and clear out feelings that you may be still carrying, feelings that are still directing you and affecting what you are now trying to accomplish. For example, if you feel you have failed and suffered a major loss, reliving the situation may help you realize that it still is affecting your actions today—either consciously or unconsciously.

The aim in clearing out the past is to now see the positive in all the things that have happened to you, understanding that who you are today is a result of how you processed what happened in the past.

If you find you have carried negative judgments that are still affecting you, it is important to discover and work on ways to change them so that you can let them go and move forward in your life. And reliving the positive things that have happened to you can give you a new perspective on how they have affected who you are today.

*Exercise Two:*

*Take the first paragraph on your negative list and ask your Higher Self the following questions:*

1. *Looking at this situation now, how do I feel it has affected who I am today?*
2. *Have I been able to see what I needed to learn from this situation?*
   - *If the answer is no, ask: What did I need to learn?*

3. *Even though it was difficult, has it helped me in some way?*

4. *After I went through this situation, was I able to let it go, or does it still affect me in some way?*
   - *If the answer is that it still affects you, ask: Why am I holding on to it?*
   - *Take that answer and ask: What do I need to do to let it go now?*

5. *When I look at what happened, do I now realize that it has had karmic consequences?'*
   - *If the answer is yes, ask: What was my karma that was connected to this?*

6. *Looking back at the situation, how would I act if it happened to me now?*
   - *Taking that answer, ask: Is there something better I should do?*
     - *If the answer is yes, ask: What is a better solution?*
     - *Taking that answer ask: Why didn't I know that solution before?*

7. *Is there something I still need to learn about this situation?*

When you review the past negative things, sometimes you realize that you haven't been aware of how they have affected who you are. It's good to come to this realization to know that you are still growing and learning.

*Exercise Three:*
   *Now take your first paragraph on the positive list and ask your Higher Self the following questions:*

1. *Looking at this situation now, do I feel it has affected who I am today?*
   - *If the answer is yes, ask: What has the main effect been?*
2. *Have I been able to see what I needed to learn from this situation?*
   - *If the answer is yes, ask: What has the main effect been?*
3. *Have I been able to see what I needed to learn from this situation?*
   - *If the answer is yes, ask: Why didn't I realize this before now?*
4. *When I look at what happened, do I realize now that it has had karmic consequences?*
   - *If the answer is yes, ask: What was my karma that was connected to this situation?*
5. *Is there anything more I need to know about what happened?*
   - *If the answer is yes, ask: Please tell me what that is?*

When you look back at the things that have happened to you in the past, realize that many of them are part of your karma, especially when it comes to relationships. See life as a series of events that shape who you are; but know that you are still in charge of making those events positive even when they start by looking like they can end up negatively.

You are the master of your own soul and the keeper of your heart and mind. Use them both well, and you will be able to change the things that challenge you and move through the obstacles that try to impede you. See yourself as a moving force that looks at life as a way to grow and prosper even in the midst of adversity. Never be afraid of the difficulties that arise or of the relationships that can cause you to feel emotional. Learn from those things that cause you sadness and rejoice in those things that give you happiness. Let go of the negative events of the past and see them now as steppingstones you needed to take to become whole.

### Chapter Four

# When Someone Finds the Path Too Difficult

This chapter is for those students who have been studying Higher Self Yoga for several years. It can also be for those who are beginners. The title denotes difficulties from the mildest to the strongest. No matter what the level of difficulty, this chapter is about when a student feels it is too much for her to continue.

Usually this feeling happens to almost everyone for a short time, one reason being that the material may cause someone to feel overwhelmed. Instead of looking at it slowly and in a planned manner, the person takes it all on at once and then comes to an impasse. To explain the best method of study is also a problem, because everyone is an individual, and what one person can do will differ from another person. This is why it's important to plan a way in which you personally can move forward.

Let's look at what I mean by this. The following are examples of study plans that may or may not be done by you. Read through them carefully and decide which one feels the most manageable to you. They will start with the most difficult to do and end with the least difficult.

1.  You read the first chapter of a book. As you do, you make a list of those things you don't understand completely. You also do each exercise and write down your answers. This you try to do in two or

three days. After you finish that chapter, you take your list of things that you don't understand, think carefully about each one, and again write down what you think it means. If you are working with a buddy or a coach, you take those questions to that person to discuss. You try to do all of this in a week, and the following week you start a new chapter.

You may also be attending a weekly class that is working on another chapter or book. You also finish the homework from that class in the same week you do the chapter from the first book.

You may also have a buddy, so you meet with your buddy once a week and work on something else that you both agree on.

Every day you also do your meditation practice and often meditate twice a day.

Obviously, doing this much work may make a person come to a standstill and get tired. This type of person usually has a strong spiritual subpersonality that influences her to do more and keep up with all the work. When she doesn't do it all, then she feels she is failing and is not a good student.

On the other hand, if the person is very disciplined, she may be able to do it all with no difficulty. It also depends on her social life. Is she in a relationship? Does she work long hours? Does she have children? All these things will be deterrents to her doing this work.

2.  At the next level of difficulty, you read and work on a chapter, also doing all the exercises. This usu-

ally takes a couple of weeks to do. You also attend a weekly class and do that work ahead of time. If you have a buddy, you will work with the buddy every two weeks on the material you choose to work on. You also do your meditation practice once and sometimes twice a day.

A lot of people can handle this level of difficulty, but again it depends on how much time they have in terms of family and work. If a person can't manage this kind of practice, unlike the person in the first example, she will feel bad but not come to a place of total discontent and feelings of failure.

3.  When you follow this next level, it feels more satisfactory in terms of living your life, socially and personally. You will try to read a book every day that you want to work with, but if you miss a day or two it doesn't bother you. You also attend a weekly class and do the assigned work for that ahead of time. Sometimes you are still too busy to do the work, but you still attend class. You have a buddy and meet either every two weeks or every three weeks. You also do try to meditate every day even if it is a short meditation.

    This practice is more acceptable to most people. Someone may follow plan two but once in a while do plan three or vise versa. In either case a person doesn't feel bad or feel she is not a good yogi if she doesn't follow through with everything in the plan.

4.  When you follow the next plan, you don't do any extra reading. If you attend a class, you do the read-

ing and the exercise, but sometimes you don't do the homework. You have a buddy and meet once every three weeks to work on something you both decide on. Once in a while you miss your buddy call. You try to meditate every day but often skip it because you are too busy.

These people basically have not made the teaching a priority. Usually, they either stay in this pattern or get worse and slip into the fifth plan. They tend to make excuses for not doing the work even when they do have the time to do it. They sometimes feel they should do more but don't really feel bad about not doing so.

5.   At this fifth level, you really have put the teaching on the back burner. Your practice is very erratic. Sometimes you read the books and do the exercises if you attend class. But often you don't do the work and sometimes don't attend class. The same is true with your buddy work. You keep changing your appointments and canceling them. When you do meet with your buddy, often you have forgotten to do the work and always have excuses, which usually are not valid. You can flow between this and the previous level and, when you get energized and do the work, sometimes the third level. But then you fall back to the fifth level until you energize yourself again and plan to change and be better.

You meditate sporadically and have difficulty, mainly because you haven't set up the vibration needed for a daily meditation practice.

This person may love the teaching but has never made it a priory; often other things—even unimportant ones—will stop her practice. She may or may not stay in the teaching, mainly because it doesn't have the importance of meaning to her that others at the higher levels feel.

These plans, of course, can change and intermix. They are simply examples of some of the practices that people do. All of them are valid. Obviously, if someone wants to grow spiritually the more difficult practices will help them the most

*Exercise One:*

*If you are a practicing yogi, look at these plans and try to identify which one you basically are doing. There can be variations from these plans, but you still should be able to determine where you are in turns of the difficult ones versus the easier ones.*

*Once you have chosen which plan you feel you are in, then ask your Higher Self the following questions:*

1. *Is my determination correct?*
   - *If the answer is yes, ask: What is the best way for me to do this?*
   - *If the answer is no, ask: Why can't I resolve it in this lifetime?*
2. *Next, ask: Do you think I can follow a more disciplined plan?*
   - *If the answer is yes, ask: Which plan should I follow, and why do you think so?*
3. *If you feel that maybe you need a less demanding plan, ask: Should I change my plan to one that is less*

*difficult? If the answer is yes, ask: What is the best way for me to do this?*

- *If the Higher Self says yes, ask: What plan would be better for me, or should I do a combination of two plans?*
- *If the answer is to do a combination of plans, ask: Please tell me what the best combination for me would be.*

4. *If you are having difficulty doing your plan, ask: How can I overcome my feelings that this is too difficult?*
5. *If you are having trouble following your plan, ask: What do I need to do to help me feel more positive about the work?*
6. *If you are feeling resistance in doing the work, ask: How can I overcome this resistance? Is there something I am not seeing?*

Sometimes someone is doing very well and being disciplined about doing the work, and then suddenly feels resistance and even anger about it. This is when you truly need to take a good look at your method. Are you doing too much? Or are you doing too little? Are your feelings coming from your lower nature or from an outside force trying to stop you? Meditate on all these questions and ask your Higher Self for help.

Some people feel they are doing well, following the plan, and even sometimes doing more than needed. Yet they may also feel they are not growing spiritually. Usually this is because they are not doing the psychological work they need. This teaching emphasizes the need to do therapy because psychological problems will keep people behind in their spiritual growth.

For example, if you have feelings of unworthiness that come from childhood conditioning, those feelings will affect you spiritually. No matter how much work you do, you will feel that it's not enough or that you aren't as good a student as someone else in the teaching. Those feelings will stop you from tackling projects; they will even keep you from doing the work or meditating. You blame your inability to follow through on something on your lack of knowledge, which is another form of unworthiness. Generally, people who feel this way about themselves lack the energy and determination to move forward on the path. Feeling unworthy is one of the factors that impede spiritual growth, but there are many others that can keep you from moving forward as well. Some of these are:

1. Lack of awareness concerning your negative characteristics that you need to change

2. Feeling dependent on the teacher to help you all the time

3. Wanting to achieve more but giving up the first time you make a mistake

4. Seeing others doing well and feeling envious, and even feeling that you are better than someone and not understanding why that person is doing better than you

5. Having the attitude that the glass is half empty instead of half full

6. Not having generosity of spirit toward others. This means living in your own world and not having the awareness of others—their needs and aspirations

7. Looking at others as competitors rather than as brothers and sisters

8. Being indolent
9. Being fearful of change
10. Having other fears that keep you from opening your heart

These are just some of the things that can stop you on the path and make your journey more difficult.

*Exercise Two:*

*Go over the above items and ask yourself if you have that trait at all. If you think you do, then ask your Higher Self if that is true, and if it is true, ask your Higher Self for a process to change it. Also, ask for a first step.*

*If you don't resonate with any of the above, then ask your Higher Self if you have any psychological problem that is keeping you from growing spiritually. If the Higher Self says yes, then ask: What is this problem? Please give me a process and a first step to change the problem.*

Sometimes the work isn't too difficult, but what is difficult is your attitude toward the work. Usually this comes from having others make demands on you, which causes you to rebel and not do anything. A teacher will test students on this characteristic in small ways. Since service is a major part of this teaching, someone who has this tendency will not want to do any service and this will stop someone's spiritual growth.

*Exercise Three:*

*Ask your Higher Self the following questions:*

1. *Do I in any way have a problem in following through on a request that someone makes of me?*

- If the answer is yes, ask: Where does this feeling of resistance come from?
- If you receive an answer, ask: How do I change this feeling?

When someone doesn't follow through, that person can develop a reputation of being someone who can't be trusted with an important mission or assignment. On the other hand, as a person grows spiritually, she will be valued because of her trustworthiness. Usually that person is given more to do as a result. If someone is a pleaser, then that person will never say no to a request, even when she hasn't the time to follow through. A trustworthy person will always determine whether she can follow through and, if she feels the request is too much for her at the time, will say no. This relates back to the importance of choosing the plan that is best for you.

As you grow spiritually, you need to make adjustments and understand what you are capable of doing without taking on too much or too little. Service for a yogi is part of the yoga tradition, but that service can vary from person to person.

Look at your life and evaluate those areas that are the most important for you to do. Plan according to your personal needs that include not only the spiritual, but also your family, friends, physical, creative activity, and entertainment that make you feel happy. Any spiritual journey should have all those things in balance. When something becomes off balance, try to adjust it. Remember Higher Self Yoga is a journey, so plan it accordingly.

### Chapter Five
# When You See Yourself Clearly

This chapter is about looking at yourself with the purpose of seeing all the positive and negative qualities you contain. You may be more aware of your negative traits and rarely see the positive ones. Self-criticism is a strong characteristic in yogis. They can feel they need to be perfect in order to grow spiritually. This is a wrong concept to have in any disciplined practice.

In the Yoga tradition, this concept comes from seeing the path not only as difficult, but also as a method to keep strict discipline, considered essential for a yogi to grow spiritually. It has been used in many ashrams, where the disciples live under ascetic conditions and have no interaction with the outside world. Living in such an environment makes perfectionism much easier to pursue, as it takes the disciple out of the normal way of living and sequesters him in an atmosphere conducive to fanaticism. This keeps the disciple from gaining knowledge of who he truly is except in these austere surroundings.

Anyone who has lived in an ashram for years and then leaves, will find himself unable to be in the world without falling out of what he may feel is grace. The challenges of life make such a person feel inadequate and lost about how to cope with all the things that happen normally to someone who hasn't been segregated in such a manner. In some cases, such a person will either find another ashram to go to or try to return to the one he left.

There is an old saying: "A yogi needs to live in the world but not be part of it." This means that a yogi has to be part of the world but not be affected by all the things that happen there. Such a person, in so doing, is able to become disidentified from his emotions so that he can observe and participate in what is happening around him with a certain degree of detachment. Such a person is compassionate, can help others, and has a deep, inner loving nature that leads him to be there when someone needs support and love. He also has a clearer understanding of life and the problems that can arise in daily living. This person understands his own strengths and weaknesses and stays focused on the issue at the time.

A yogi who lives in the world has more challenges in terms of his practice, but if he lives up to the challenges and sees them in a disidentified manner, then he is walking the true path of the yogi.

The following story illustrates what I am saying:

Jane entered an ashram when she was eighteen. Her guru was an East Indian who had moved to the States when he was in his mid-forties. Before that, he had been a guru in India until his teacher told him to take his teaching to America and start an ashram there.

When Jane was thirty, a huge scandal happened at the ashram. A number of women who were close to the guru accused him of having sexually molested them. When the accusations were confirmed, the ashram community cast him out. Many of the disciples also left and Jane was one of them.

Jane had developed skills at the ashram and was soon able to find a job nearby. She also found a small but nice apartment, with Laura, another disciple. They were friends and had done some projects together in the ashram, but once they were on their own, they found there was little they had in common. Laura was thirty when she had entered the ashram and was there for only five years, in contrast to Jane's twelve. Adjusting to the world was much easier for Laura. She had made friends previously and quickly returned to the social life she had before. She even was able to get another job in her former firm.

Jane, on the other hand, was at a complete loss in terms of being in the world. She tried to continue her spiritual practice in the morning and in the evening after work. Laura was going out a lot, so at first it worked out well for Jane; but when Laura brought some of her friends home—including a male friend—Jane's meditation practice was interrupted.

Laura invited her to go out with her socially, and Jane did so a couple of times, but she felt awkward and didn't participate in any of the conversations. She considered going back to the ashram, which was still functioning with outside programs for the community, but that didn't feel right, either. Laura found out that the new leaders at the ashram were paying for therapy to help the disciples, many of whom were going through trauma about what had happened. She talked Jane into getting this help.

Jane started therapy and began to see that a lot of her beliefs were based on her childhood conditioning. She realized that wanting to live in an ashram stemmed from inner fears of being in relationships. Living in the world was frightening because it meant having to relate to others. Slowly, over a year, Jane started to make friends, first at work, and then in sometimes joining Laura when she went to parties. Jane loved art and started to go to art openings and even decided to take an art class and learn to paint.

Men found Jane to be very attractive—she was petite with big brown eyes and a sweet disposition. They started asking her out, but it felt too strange and awkward to her, as she never had dated, even in high school.

Her therapist focused on this issue, and finally Jane accepted a date with Andy, a man she had met at an art opening, who was warm-hearted and easy to talk to.

She still meditated and continued her spiritual practice, but not as fanatically as before. Her challenge of being in the world and not of it still existed; but over time she was able to adjust to life and, in the adjustment, realize that she could still grow spiritually and have a stronger understanding about herself, her needs, and her true beliefs.

To have a clear understanding of yourself requires an awareness that takes practice. I would suggest you do the following:

*Exercise One:*
1. *Make a list of all your negative characteristics. Be honest and include any that anyone has ever mentioned to you, whether you believed the person or not.*
2. *Then make a list of all your positive characteristics. Again, be honest and include any that anyone has ever mentioned to you.*
3. *Now prioritize both lists: on your negative list, put your worst characteristic first; on your positive list, put your best characteristic first.*

It's important when you make these lists to determine how the characteristic makes you feel. If it is a negative trait, after you have acted it out, do you feel bad, or do you try to justify it? If it is a positive trait, does it make you feel good, or do you just ignore it?

Some of your characteristics you may not care about. For example, you may talk too loudly if you get excited, and you think that is fine, but it might not be fine if you are talking to someone whom you feel has wronged you.

Think about each characteristic in terms of how it may affect others. For example, shouting at someone may make the person afraid or just angry and defensive. Expressing positive feelings to someone may make that person feel happy or possibly embarrassed.

Obviously, your personality, which encompasses all your characteristics, will affect different people in their own unique ways. You may say something that could be interpreted as a critical remark to one person and another person may feel what you've said as something that is helpful to know. Usually this depends on the tone of your voice as well as the exact words.

Using a harsh voice can make a remark sound critical, while the same thing said in a soft, caring voice can sound helpful. For example, if you say in a strong tone, "You upset me when you do that, so stop it!" the other person will feel defensive. If, on the other hand, you say in a nice tone of voice, "When you do that I feel upset; I would appreciate it if you would be aware of how it affects me and try not do it," the other person will be more receptive. The exchange could even result in a conversation that is positive for both of you.

Now take both lists and check them with your Higher Self, asking if your lists and priorities are correct. Also ask if there is something that is missing from your lists that needs to be added. Usually people don't credit themselves with more positive characteristics. Also ask if there is something on the lists that shouldn't be there? When you feel the lists are correct do the following exercise. Start with the top negative characteristic.

*Exercise Two:*
  *Once you have chosen which plan you feel you are in then ask your Higher Self the following questions:*

1.  *Are my feelings about this characteristic correct?*
    - *If the answer is no, ask: Why not?*
      - *Taking that answer, ask: Is there a reason I'm not aware of this?*
2.  *Do I want to change this characteristic?*
    - *If the answer is no, ask: Why not?*
    - *If the answer is yes, ask: What is my first step?*
3.  *Is this a characteristic I learned in childhood?*
    - *If the answer is yes, ask: What were the circumstances?*
    - *If the answer is no, ask: Where and when did I learn it?*
    - *If you believe in reincarnation, ask: Did I bring this characteristic in from a previous lifetime*
      - *If the answer is yes, ask: Can I know more about the life or lifetimes?*
4.  *Do I have any pre-knowledge of when I start to be in this characteristic?*
    - *If the answer is no, ask: Why not? And how can I be more aware of this?*
    - *If the answer is yes, ask: Is there a way I can stop myself from being in it?*
5.  *Does a certain person in my life cause me to be in this characteristic?*
    - *If the answer is yes, ask: Who is the person?*
      - *Then ask: What about the person causes me to act this way?*
6.  *Do certain situations bring out this characteristic?*
    - *If the answer is yes, ask: What are they?*
7.  *Do I feel a certain way when I get into this characteristic?*

- *If the answer is yes, ask: What is it and how can I stop it?*

Usually when someone is feeling negative it is caused by preexisting circumstances.

Someone could be feeling very tired or even feeling ill. He could be irritated about something that happened previously, with a person, work, or physical endeavor. Some people are very moody and blow up at the least provocation. Such a person is not only difficult to live, with but obviously needs psychological help.

If you are having any of these feelings, it's important not to interact with people until you can rest and feel calm. Most problems are caused by overreactions about something that isn't very important. If you feel it is important to talk to someone about something, be certain you are clear headed, calm and understand the emotions of the circumstance. Too often people get into arguments when something could be resolved in a positive manner. If you live with someone, the chances of your negative characteristics coming up with the person are very high. It's good to talk about it with the person. Be honest about your relationship, about what is good, and what needs to be better.

Sometimes someone will also take his negative characteristics to his work; and if he is in a management position, use them on his employees. Children can also be a target for someone with negative emotions.

If any of your negative traits are extreme or you have trouble controlling them, then you definitely need therapeutic help. Often this situation comes about from having had an abusive childhood

*Exercise Three:*
  *It is time to work with your top positive characteristic. Ask*

*your Higher Self the following questions:*

1.  *Are my feelings concerning this characteristic correct?*
    *   *If the answer is no, ask: Why not?*
        *   *Taking that answer, ask: Is there a reason I'm not aware of this?*
2.  *Do I want to enhance this characteristic?*
    *   *If the answer is no, ask: Why not?*
    *   *If the answer is yes, you do want to enhance this, ask: What is my first step in doing this?*
3.  *Is this a characteristic that I learned in childhood?*
    *   *If the answer is yes, ask: What were the circumstances?*
    *   *If the answer is no, ask: Where and when did I learn it?*
    *   *If you believe in reincarnation, ask: Did I bring this characteristic in from a previous lifetime?*
        *   *If the answer is yes, ask: Can I know more about the life or lifetimes?*
4.  *Is this characteristic one that I should be using more than I do?*
    *   *If yes, ask: Why am I not using it more?*
    *   *If the answer is yes, ask: What more do I have to do?*
5.  *Does a certain person in my life cause me to be in this characteristic?*
    *   *If the answer is yes, ask: Who is the person?*
    *   *Then ask: What about the person causes me to act this way?*
6.  *Do certain situations cause me to be in this characteristic?*

- *If the answer is yes, ask: What are they?*
7. *Do I feel a certain way when I get into this characteristic?*
   - *If the answer is yes, ask: How do I feel, and should I try to enhance the feeling?*

It is very important when you work with a negative trait that you also work at the same time with a positive one. There should be positive characteristics on your list that you have but don't use very much. When you work with them, try to develop them more and try also to have the awareness that you can do this.

There also may be characteristics that you admire and would like to have. Add them to your list, and ask your Higher Self for a process for you to follow so you can bring them into your consciousness. You may discover that you have such a characteristic, but it is dormant. When you start working with it, it may suddenly emerge and be easy to develop.

When you work with negative characteristics, take just one at a time to work with, and continue working with it until you feel your awareness is helping you to not engage in it. The same is true when you work with the positive list. Take one characteristic at a time until you understand and feel yourself naturally being in it.

This work obviously will take time. Try not to overdo it, and also do not be self-critical if a negative characteristic is difficult to change. The same is true with a positive characteristic. If you are trying to enhance it and are having a difficult time doing this, realize that even a positive characteristic is difficult to develop.

Initially working with this chapter will help you see yourself more clearly. On the yoga path, it's always important to understand who you are, and it helps you also to be more aware of the changes you go through in your spiritual growth.

### Chapter Six

## Looking at the Way You See Others

Often when one person encounters another, she will see that person from her own set of standards and often miss an opportunity of knowing someone very special. The tendency is to be attracted to someone who is similar to yourself and reject someone who has not only a different personality but also a different appearance—one that you may feel is very strange.

This kind of response usually results in not furthering the acquaintanceship. Much is lost by societal standards that segregate people into groups. Generally, a cultured person will reject someone whom she feels is uncultured. Or, for example, someone may meet a person from another culture, a person who dresses differently and has an unfamiliar accent. The other person may be highly educated and knowledgeable but lacks the social standards you expect. Even if that person is outgoing and would like to be accepted, if she is too different, you may not want to include her in your circle of friends.

Sometimes, someone will invite a friend to a special occasion, and not want to stay with the person, but instead visit with other people—leaving the friend on her own. If the friend is outgoing, she will introduce herself to others; but if she is shy, she may find a place to hide and wait for the person to come back and rescue her. This will cause the friend not to want to go out with the person. Friendship can be broken because of such lack of awareness.

People often neglect to be cordial to strangers, but find excuses not to like someone when the person hasn't done anything wrong, and is simply trying to make herself accepted.

Also, when someone is born into a wealthy family, she may consider herself better than others and will not befriend someone who comes from a poor family. Even when there isn't a caste system like the one in India, in Western countries, there is what could be called a hidden caste system, where the wealthy only befriend the wealthy, and the poor befriend the poor. The main difference between the two is that in the West, the poor can do well and can then enter the wealthy domain. But sometimes when that happens, there is still no acceptance by the older families of wealth who comprise the aristocracy of society.

This sort of discrimination has existed for centuries, even in democratic countries, and it causes prejudices and hatred that are passed down from generation to generation. Unfortunately, it still strongly exists in most countries where people judge others by their religion or by the color of their skin. Where equality is meant to prevail, there is bigotry and distrust. Where loving your neighbors is meant to happen, there is hatred and discord.

Another prejudice that people have comes from past lives. Often there is strong negative karma in families. This can exist between a parent and a child, or among siblings. Also, someone may meet a person that she dislikes right away, or she may become romantically involved with someone, and only to find the relationship becomes confrontational and negative. Marriages often dissolve because of this.

The reason I am writing this chapter is to also say that yogis, who are meant to love one another and be kindhearted, also often carry prejudices within them. Mainly, the prejudice comes from having had a negative past life with someone. This feeling of dislike carries over and can affect a relationship either immediately or at a later time. The people involved may be very different from when they had interactions in a previous life. There may have been many lifetimes of learning in between, but the feelings can still remain the same, as the following story illustrates

Pedro, a young man in his late twenties, met his teacher, Alex, in New York City. Alex was a Western guru who had classes in several cities throughout the United States and traveled yearly to teach the students there. The two had met when Pedro was visiting a friend, who was a disciple, and Pedro had gone with him to Alex's class. Pedro knew right away that Alex was his teacher and asked to study with him. Alex said that he had a class in Pedro's city, Cleveland, Ohio, and he wrote a letter for Pedro to take to the leader of the class when he returned home.

When Pedro went to the class in Cleveland, he felt like a stranger and didn't feel the same welcoming energy he felt when he had gone to the New York class. There were only ten people in the class and he soon found out that he was the first newcomer in several years; the rest of them had all been together for a long time.

Pedro was very intelligent; he had a Ph.D. in science and worked for a major company. He also was studying art as a hobby and had read many books on philosophy and religion. There were several people his same age in the class, and he reached out to them inviting them to his home for a social evening. Two accepted and the others declined for various reasons. The two who came seemed friendly enough, but Pedro realized they didn't have much in common. However, they were much more knowledgeable about the teaching, and he thought he could learn from them. He also tried to get closer to some of the others in class as well, but only one person, Helen, was receptive and warm-hearted.

He kept attending class on a regular basis, but more and more felt the other people in the class didn't want him to be there. John, the leader of the class, especially acted sometimes in a hostile manner toward him, and Pedro felt John could be influencing the others against him.

He finally confronted John about it, and John said that a yogi doesn't have to love everybody in the teaching that naturally he was closer to those people who had been in the class longer. He also told Pedro that he always acted as if he were smarter than the rest. Pedro, said that he didn't know that he acted that way and apologized.

Pedro told Helen about their conversation, and asked her if what John said about him was true.

She said, "I have never seen you act that way, but I have noticed the way John acts toward you. Maybe he is jealous of your intellectual accomplishments, or there could just be some bad karma between the two of you.

"I understand about karma," Pedro said, "but I would think a yogi would recognize bad karma, and even if there were problems in a previous life, a yogi wouldn't be influenced them, especially someone like John, who is more advanced."

"That's not necessarily true. Karma acts in strange ways. Someone could have learned to be conscious of karma and even feel free of it, and then, without awareness, suddenly be hit by it and surrender to it. My advice is to talk to our teacher about it."

Pedro called Alex and told him what was happening and what Helen had said.

Alex agreed that it sounded like John and Pedro had a difficult past life together, and that was causing John's behavior. He was surprised that John hadn't realized what was happening and said, "Even when a disciple is advanced, he can get caught up in karma, and not realize what is happening. I am coming to your city soon and will set up a time for the three of us to talk about this."

When Alex arrived, he had John and Pedro sit down and face one another, really look into each other eyes, and then ask their Higher Selves if they have been together before in a previous life. If they had, what was their relationship and how did it end?

They both saw in their meditation that they had been brothers. John was the elder and Pedro the youngest. Their family was very wealthy and in the English society. Their father disliked John and psychologically abused him, constantly telling him that he wasn't as smart as his brother. This caused John not only to dislike his father, but also to hate his brother and play mean tricks on him. Their mother also preferred Pedro, making John's life even worse. When his father died, instead of leaving his estate to John, he only gave him a small amount and left the rest to Pedro. John left England, went to America, and died in the Revolutionary war.

This experience explained John's feeling of jealousy and dislike toward Pedro, and Pedro's feeling of not being wanted or accepted in the class.

Knowing this made their relationship more cordial, and also made the rest of the class more accepting of Pedro. As John had previously said, the two would never love each other or be close friends, but they could be good spiritual brothers.

The above story happens often in spiritual classes. In some instances, a person will leave because of the lack of welcome. Especially in ashrams where the disciples have lived for many years, when a new student joins and has the attention of the guru, it can cause discord among those who have been there a long time.

Not everyone's personality will be received positively in any group. People are individuals and too often there is discord especially if a new person finds favoritism with the leader. Jealousy is very dominant in all organizations. It's always important to see a person with new eyes and not be judgmental, even when you feel the person is saying or doing something that you don't like. Mainly be open, stay focused on what is happening, and be disidentified when it comes to any disagreements between others.

It's always best to be in your heart when you talk to others and if you are involved in a conflict of any kind, always link with your Higher Self and ask that it guide you. The following exercise is to determine your feeling when meeting someone new whom you immediately dislike.

*Exercise One:*

*Ask your Higher Self the following questions::*

1. *Am I welcoming to new people coming into my life in any way?*
   - *If the answer is no, ask: Why not?*
2. *When I am in a group of people, do I try to talk to those people I do not know?*
   - *If the answer is no, ask: Why not?*
3. *If I meet someone for whom I have feelings of dislike, do I try to understand why I feel that way?*
   - *If the answer is no, ask: Why not?*
4. *Do I have any personal prejudices toward a specific race or culture?*
   - *If the answer is yes, from your family, ask: How can I start to let those prejudices go?*
5. *Also ask: Is there a part of me that wants to hold on to some prejudices?*
   - *If the answer is yes, ask: Why?*

It is very important to be aware of your feelings toward others. You may have a friend who dislikes someone you both know, and that friend's dislike will affect your own feelings toward the person. This dynamic also takes place with family members. Usually a family will include several people who dislike each other, and often that can split a family into pieces. Some family members will even refuse to see certain others and be very upset if you don't follow their directions.

This behavior, of course, comes from old karmic ties that ended badly. Unfortunately, these people will keep coming back together until they resolve the karma.

### Chapter Seven

# Seeing Yourself as a Yogi

Why is it important to see yourself as a yogi? That may be the first question you are asking. Once you are committed to this teaching, there are many reasons why it is important to realize what it means for you to be a yogi. The reasons are the following:

1.  To acknowledge that you are a yogi is to acknowledge that you are now on the path seeking God Consciousness.

2.  Being a yogi means you need to see yourself completely—all your negative characteristics as well as all your positive characteristics.

3.  Once you have more awareness of who you truly are, then you need to start the process of transmuting the negative and enhancing the positive. This is a very difficult commitment, one that can require many years.

4.  When I say commitment, I mean just that. Being a yogi means you have to commit yourself to following the path, no matter where it takes you.

5.  It's important, once you are on the path, to begin the process of understanding the origins and guidelines of the teaching and how to follow them in order to grow spiritually.

6.  A yogi is also someone who cares about what is happening in his community, in his state, in his country,

and in the world and is open to fighting for just causes.

7. A yogi always does some form of service that benefits others.

8. A yogi's purpose, when he is advanced, is to teach and help others to grow spiritually.

9. When a yogi goes through initiations, it is important that he become a warrior. A warrior has no fears, is courageous, and follows his Higher Self in all things.

10. A yogi's goal is to become one with his Higher Self.

*Exercise One:*

*Look at the ten steps and ask yourself the following questions about each one:*

1. *Can I accept this?*
   - *If the answer is no, ask why not?*
2. *Take that answer and ask your Higher Self:*
   - *How can I start to change this?*

Of course, there are many steps along the way that require a yogi to learn discernment, understanding of others, and mainly how to use his heart and mind together in everything he does. Fortunately, a yogi has a teacher who will always be there for him, and that relationship will help a yogi always to feel protected and cared for. Too often a yogi forgets that he is being helped in the subtle world and that he is being watched during his spiritual transitioning both there and in the world.

When someone enters a spiritual teaching, whether it is a yoga teaching or some other esoteric teaching, he has entered a path that requires him to walk forward, develop spiritual abilities, and strive toward reaching the end where he can become a high initiate. The path is full of obstacles that relate to the person, and it is also full of challenges that require the person to go through changes, some of which are unexpected and difficult. Learning to be a yogi is part of a spiritual journey that often is started in one life and sometimes takes several lifetimes to complete.

It is not important to think about time. It doesn't matter if it takes a long time to finish the path or a short time; what matters is the ability to learn how to tread the path with a deep awareness of your personal process. The following story illustrates this point:

Brigette, a woman in her early thirties, lived in a house next to several acres of community woods with trails. She had spent a lot of time walking on them in the summer and skiing on them in the winter. Strong and athletic, Brigette felt she had explored every path and knew where it would take her; but surprisingly, one summer morning she saw a narrow path she hadn't been on before. She decided to follow it to its end; but as she walked, unexpected things began to happen to her.

First, she came upon a fallen tree, and she had to walk through some thick undergrowth to get around it. Once she had succeeded, she continued along the path until she was stopped at a stream that had a log across it. The log barely touched the other side, but she decided to try walking across on it anyway.

Unfortunately, she slipped into the water and had to crawl out. It was a hot day, so the water wasn't too cold; but Brigette was a bit shaken by the fall and sat there for a few minutes to recover. Looking back down the stream, she realized that if she had walked a little to the left, there was a footbridge she could have crossed. Always in a hurry, she neglected to first investigate to see if there was a better way across. Well, at least she could take that detour going back.

At this point Brigette was thinking that maybe it would be better to do just that—go back now rather than continue on the path. But she had a strong will to finish anything she started, so she persisted onward. Again, she was stopped. This time there was a rock formation that had fallen from the hill that was beside it. It wasn't big but had some oddly shaped stones that made it difficult for her to climb.

Brigette managed to get to the top and saw that going down on the other side was very steep, and the stones had wet moss on them, which surely would make them slippery. She looked down the rocks on either side of the path, and realized they didn't seem to stop anywhere for her to cross more easily. She realized that continuing was impossible and felt very disillusioned.

It was past noon, so Brigette sat down to eat a sandwich she had brought with her.

As she sat, she decided it was best to turn back and not try to continue. As she got up to go down the way she had come, she heard a sound and saw a deer running down the path. When it reached the rocks, it turned left and ran off through the woods. Turning around she looked down the steep slope and saw the deer running toward her on the path from where she had just come. When it reached the rocks, it turned left and ran off through the woods. This meant there had to be a clearing where you could get through the rocks. When she got down to the bottom of the rocks, she turned in the same direction as the deer and walked through the woods. Suddenly she saw a clearing in between the trees that she could easily get through.

Brigette was able to get back on the path and follow it. It now seemed like a straight easy path with no obstacles. There were tall trees lining the way and even some wild lowers peeking up here and there through the terrain. Feeling a bit tired, Brigette sat down on a large rock to rest and enjoyed the sun that was shining through the leaves. She even closed her eyes and had a short meditation. Suddenly, her inner vision clouded over, and a dark figure in a hooded robe appeared and in a deep, penetrating voice said, "Go back! It's too dangerous for you to continue on the path."

She quickly opened her eyes but didn't see anyone there. Being in the woods had always delighted her, but now, for the first time, Brigette felt afraid and started imagining all the things that could harm her. She had seen bears before in the woods and thought maybe there was a bear that would attack her or some other fierce animal, like a coyote. It was still very early, but if she got lost, she might not get back before dark. Her mind conjured up other dangerous things that could happen to her. Finally, a part in her said, "Stop it! That figure was a dark illusion trying to make you afraid. Stop listening to it!"

Taking some deep breaths, she got up and continued down the path. The path narrowed and in some places was difficult to follow. Brigette had a compass and kept track of the direction in which she was going, so if she got lost, she could relocate the right direction. She also had her cell phone so she could always call for help if she needed to.

Somehow now her determination was even stronger; nothing could make her give up and go back until she reached the end of the path. When she encountered other barriers, she got through them, not easily, but by taking her time and checking all the possibilities. Finally, the path broadened and came to a major path, one that she recognized. It took her out of the woods to a road that led back to her house.

This story shows that on the spiritual path there will be obstacles, but there will also be help, such as the deer. There will be those who will cause you to be afraid and doubt, but if you have the commitment and strive to overcome the challenges, with the help of your Higher Self, you can reach your goal. It takes courage, determination, striving, and working with your Higher Self to help you move forward. The path is there. Following it will show you beauty, wisdom, and also your negativity. Tread it carefully and know that you will always be helped.

*Exercise Two:*

*Think about the spiritual path and those areas in your life that you feel can become obstacles or challenges for you. Write them down. After you have your list, check all the ones you put down with your Higher Self to verify that they are obstacles or challenges.*

1. *Then ask your Higher Self: Are there any obstacles or challenges I will be discovering in the future that I have not previously been aware of and that aren't on my list?*
   - *If the answer is yes, ask: Can you tell me what they are?*
     - *Take that answer and add the new obstacles and challenges to your list.*

If the answer is no, the Higher Self cannot tell you what those obstacles or challenges will be, it's important to realize that they will keep coming up as you live your life. Also, what is an obstacle or challenge now may not be one if it comes up later, and what happens later in your life can cause obstacles and challenges that are not apparent now.

The only things you can work on now are those things that you are aware of that can cause you to be stuck on the path.

*Exercise Three:*

*Next, prioritize the list, making the most difficult challenge number one. Beginning with the most difficult, ask your Higher Self the following questions:*

1. *Is this challenge something that came from this life?*
   - *If the answer is yes, ask: Tell me when and where it came from?*
2. *If the answer is no, and you believe in past lives, ask: Did this come from a past life?*
   - *If the answer is yes, ask: Tell me when and where it came from?*
3. *Again, taking the first one, ask: Is this something I can easily overcome?*
   - *If the answer is no, it won't be easy to overcome, ask: Can you tell me why?*
4. *Also ask: What is my first step to try to work with this challenge and get through it?*
5. *Then ask: Is there someone who can help me in this process?*

Know that this is indeed a process. As you work with each obstacle or challenge on your list, you may find that certain ones may change into something bigger or harder to overcome, or you may find that some will not be difficult at all once you start working with them. Remember, your life will be changing as you grow spiritually.

You may feel strongly about some of the issues on your list at this time, and later they may not be a problem. There will also be issues you are handling now with ease that can change and cause you to feel blocked later on.

The spiritual path is also not always difficult. There will be times when you experience feelings of happiness and joy. Live in those moments, and know that when you encounter the opposite, striving to go through those hardships will always bring you to a place where you feel peace and beauty.

The spiritual path takes you into areas of the unknown where you will start to understand the meaning of existence and why evolution always ends in the highest realms. There will be others who come with you who will be your brothers and sisters, and others who have gone before you who will help you. There also will be times when you will help those who follow you, who will continue the spiritual journey in your footsteps. Know the value of this journey and the adventure that is before you. Your teachers are there for you to turn to, and they will teach you how to walk through the wilderness.

### Chapter Eight

# When You See Your Personality Clearly

The previous chapter was about the obstacles and challenges yogis have to meet when they walk the spiritual path. This chapter is about how you see yourself on that path and whether you see yourself clearly, in terms of all the things that happen in your life to prevent you from walking the path in the first place. A yogi's journey is never easy, but it becomes more difficult if the person doesn't evaluate her progress as she continues down the path.

Knowing the obstacles and challenges as they occur is fine, but there is another issue that also needs awareness and understanding. That issue is knowing yourself completely, not just in terms of self-awareness, which was talked about in Chapter Five, where you looked at all your negative and positive characteristics. What I mean in this chapter is knowing yourself in terms of your personality and in terms of your life goals. It's also important to understand how others see you. Sometimes a person has no awareness of how she appears to others, and in fact, may believe she appears a certain way, but actually appears very differently. Too often a person thinks of herself as being very centered and steady in her mannerisms and does not see that she may appear scattered and unorganized to others. The following is a story about this:

Gianna was a woman in her early fifties. She had been studying the teaching since she was in her early twenties and was a very devoted disciple to her teacher. Her major problem in the teaching was her lack of awareness concerning her personality. She was diligent in doing her spiritual practice—meditating daily, attending class, and doing service in her community. Unfortunately, she wasn't progressing in the teaching and had only received two initiations during all that time.

When she asked her teacher why this was happening and what was wrong, he replied that she needed be more aware of how she appeared to others and that some of her mannerisms needed to improve. This surprised Gianna, and she asked him what mannerisms she needed to improve. He replied, "When you talk to others you sometimes can sound condescending."

This reply shocked her, and she said, "But I love my brothers and sisters. I think I sound loving when I talk to them."

"Well, you sound loving with certain people who are your closest friends, but not with some of the others."

"Have people said this to you?" She was thinking, since I'm close to my teacher, they may be saying these things to him out of jealousy.

"No, I have observed this myself." He added, "You tend to be moody, and can sound condescending when you are feeling down."

"Really! I thought that when I was around you I was always positive."

"Sometimes a person doesn't see or hear how she sounds. It's important to be more aware of those aspects about yourself."

Gianna left him feeling very dejected. She really didn't understand what he meant and couldn't see herself acting in the ways he suggested.

When she went out with some friends later that week, she asked them if she ever acted moody and negative toward them. They told her that it was okay; they were used to her sometimes being a little offensive and just figured she was in a bad mood that day. They knew she worked at a difficult job and understood that sometimes it brought her down.

Again, Gianna was surprised and started to think back on some of her relationships, particularly with the men she had dated. She had never wanted to get married but had lived with a couple of men for several years. They certainly were not easy to live with, and she had been the one to break up with them. Now, she thought about some of the things that had gone wrong during those times. She was always quick to be judgmental when they did something wrong, but so were they. In fact, she walked out on the last one when he started accusing her of not understanding him and not being there for him when he needed her. Another one, in fact, told her she was making too many demands on him. The first relationship had ended with both feeling it was over and time to move on. The last affair, which was five years ago, lasted longer and ended badly with lots of arguments and denunciations. It had made her feel too vulnerable to consider looking for someone else since then.

It was true that her job, which was working as an account executive in an advertising company, was difficult and time consuming; but she loved it, and there was no reason for her to feel moody when it made her tired.

Gianna then talked to her family, and they confirmed what the others had said, adding that she had been that way since she was a little kid. This made her realize that maybe this moody and condescending part of her personality had come in with her from a previous life.

She asked her teacher if she had brought some of these personality traits in from a past life. He meditated about it and said yes, she had been a man who was in charge of a large estate with many peasants working for him. She had acquired a dominating personality in her job of overseeing them.

When she knew more about her personality in that former life, Gianna realized that she was projecting some of it on to her friends and spiritual brothers and sisters. Gianna apologized to them and asked everyone to point it out to her when she fell back into that personality. Slowly, she started to correct herself and started to grow more spiritually.

No one has a perfect personality. Also, very few people recognize the aspects of their personality that need changing. Mostly, when someone knows a person, she accepts the personality—the good and the bad—and rarely tells the person about how she sounds and appears. Obviously, if someone has a terrible personality, that person will not be able to make many friends. Unfortunately, such a person hasn't the awareness to look at herself and make changes to become more acceptable to others. Usually such a person blames others for not befriending her.

It's best to evaluate yourself sincerely—your good traits as well as the negative ones—in how you interact with others, in terms both of friends and of people you know casually. What follows are lists of personality traits, both positive and negative.

The first list is of positive traits.
1. Being warm-hearted toward others
2. Being friendly when meeting someone new
3. Having the ability to notice if someone needs physical help
4. Being aware if someone needs emotional help
5. Noticing other people's moods at any given time
6. Seeing others in a way that is generally positive
7. When you aren't feeling well, trying not to talk about it to others

8.  If you are feeling emotional about something, not projecting that on to others

9.  Looking at situations in a disidentified manner

10. Taking action when it is needed in a difficult situation

11. Including others in a conversation with a group of people

12. In a meeting or at a party, noticing if someone is alone and not mingling and helping that person to join others

13. Being aware of your moods and, if you are feeling irritated, withdrawing from conversations until you are past the mood

14. Keeping out of arguments with someone who attacks you, withdrawing from the person if possible

15. In conversations, always trying to mirror the person if she needs help

16. Never dominating a conversation if there are several people talking

17. Trying to be in your heart when talking to someone

18. Remembering to link with your Higher Self when you start a conversation with someone, whether in person or on the phone

19. If you love someone, trying to send that love to that person when you talk to him or her

20. Thinking before you speak, so that the words are kind and loving and correct in the situation

This is a general list of positive traits. If you think of any more you want to add to this list, do that now.

*Exercise One:*

*Look at the list, one item at a time, and rate yourself from one to ten, ten meaning you have this trait most of the time.*

*After you have done so, check your rating for each item with your Higher Self. If the Higher Self doesn't agree with your rating, ask:*

*How would you rate this issue?*

*When the true rating has been determined, take those items that have ratings from one to five. Beginning with your top item with the lowest rating, ask the Higher Self the following questions:*

1. *Is there a reason I haven't developed this positive trait?*
   - *If the answer is yes, ask: What is the reason?*
   - *Take that answer and ask: How can I change this? Give me a process and a first step*
2. *If there isn't any reason for not having this positive trait, ask: How can I best start to develop this positive trait?*

Work in this way with one trait at a time. When you feel you are using that trait more often, move on to the next one.

You may also want to take those traits that you rated five to eight, and with each one, ask your Higher Self how you can improve it and raise the rating to nine or ten.

There also may be some traits that you prefer to work with first because they feel more important to you. If this is the case, prioritize your list, putting the ones that you want to work with the most on top.

When you work with this list try to imagine you are using this trait with someone you know. If you actually did use this trait with someone, remember the scene, and see the interaction between the two of you. If you don't recall such a scene, make one up and imagine how you would play out this trait.

It's good for some people to visualize the action from above, looking down at themselves and the other person or persons.

Either way, letting yourself experience the trait gives you a better understanding of how it feels when you enact it. The more that happen, the more you become accustomed to doing it until it becomes a natural part of your personality.

The next personality traits you will work with are the negative ones. Some of them can be the following:

1. Not listening to someone who is talking to you or others
2. Obviously pretending to be interested when someone is talking about what she is doing
3. Acting distracted when someone is talking to you.
4. Not being aware when someone is feeling sad or unhappy
5. Trying to make a good impression, but messing up because of nerves
6. Acting overly emotional about something
7. Being accusatory toward someone in a nasty way
8. Not being helpful when someone needs help
9. Looking at situations in a egoistic manner
10. Being demanding
11. Not being cordial to a new person
12. Not being disciplined when something is expected of you
13. Making excuses for not following through on something you were meant to do

14. Using your personality to be overly charming and manipulative

15. Looking at everything that happens as to whether it supports your ego needs

16. Being self-consumed and selfish

17. Seeing others as challenges and sometimes unworthy of your friendship.

18. Being authoritarian, especially with loved ones

19. Always wanting to have more

20. Complaining about things that are happening to you or around you

This is just a general list of negative traits. If you think of any more that you want to add to this list do that now.

*Exercise Two:*

*Look at the list, one item at a time, and rate yourself from one to ten, ten meaning you have this trait most of the time.*

*After you have done so, check your rating for each item with your Higher Self. If the Higher Self doesn't agree with your rating, ask: How would you rate this issue?*

*When the true rating has been determined, take those items that have ratings from five to ten. Beginning with your top item with the highest rating, ask the Higher Self the following:*

  *1. Is there a reason I have this negative trait?*
     • *If the answer is yes, ask: What is the reason?*
  *2. Did I develop this trait in my childhood?*
     • *If the answer is yes, ask: What were the circum-stances?*
  *3. If you believe in past lives, ask: Did I bring this trait in from a past life?*

- *If the answer is yes, ask: Can you tell me more about it?*
4. *Is this trait something that I truly would like to change?*
   - *If the answer is no, ask: Why not?*
5. *Does having this trait give me something I need?*
   - *If the answer is yes, ask: Can you tell me more about it?*
6. *If you are ready to work on changing this trait, ask: What is a process and a first step?*

Work this list one trait at a time. When you feel you are now enacting that one less often, move on to the next one. You may also want to work on those traits that you rated three to five: with each one, ask your Higher Self how you can lower its rating to zero or one.

There may be some traits you prefer to work with first because they feel more important. If that is the case, prioritize your list by putting the items you most want to work with on top.

When you work with this list try to imagine you are using this trait with someone you know. If you actually did express this trait with someone, remember the scene, and see the interaction between the two of you. If you don't recall such a scene, make one up and imagine it happening and how you would play out this trait.

It's good for some people to visualize the action from above looking down at themselves and the other person or persons.

Either way, letting yourself experience the trait gives you a better understanding of how it feels when you enact it. The more that happens, the more you can stop doing it until it is no longer a part of your personality.

Changing your personality in any way takes time and diligence. Remember your personality traits are something you have had for many years and in some cases for many lifetimes. Be kind with yourself and non-judgmental. Always recognize the positive aspects of your personality as much as the negative ones. Remember also that you are not perfect, nor is anyone else. Being perfect is not good to strive for. It causes fanaticism and discord. Your personality reflects who you are. Striving to be in your heart will bring you closer to others and make you happier in your daily life.

### Chapter Nine

## When You See Yourself at a Crossroads

When I talk about being at a crossroads, it can mean many things. Most people feel that it means coming to a place in your life where you need to make a decision concerning which direction to go in. It means choosing which one is better and deciding to travel in that direction. It usually happens around turning points in your life, such as determining what college to go to, what vocation to decide on, or whether to get married or not. It can also concern picking a spiritual direction.

Basically, a crossroads always involves a difficult decision to make. A person frequently gets stuck there and can't decide which way to go. Sometimes, if a person does decide to go in a certain direction, she may later want to turn back and go the other way.

Being in such a place in your life can be life-changing to such a degree that it will affect you for many years and often can affect the rest of your life. When the decision is a wrong one, it can cause someone to leave her destiny and lose what it was meant to be. The following story illustrates this.

Jamal was a very intelligent man. At age thirty-six, he was well established in his career as an engineer and was planning to marry a woman he had been dating for several years.

Sometimes he was very happy with the life he was living—with his work, his friends, and his loved one—but once in a while he would become upset and moody. When he was in this frame of mind, everything in his life seemed wrong. These moods would last for a day or two and usually ended with his becoming determined to go back to his feelings of life being wonderful.

When Ayanna, his fiancé, saw him in such a mood, she disappeared. Originally, when he was in the doldrums, she would try to help him; but he always rejected her best effort and even acted a bit nasty to her.

Usually, these moods would happen once a month, but they started to occur on a more regular basis and lasted longer. Jamal tried to make excuses for them, but finally, even he had to admit that something was wrong. He finally listened to Ayanna's urges and went to see a psychiatrist, who put Jamal on anti-depressant medications, but they made him feel tired all the time to the extent he was finding it difficult to do his work. Other medications were prescribed, but none of them seemed to help.

He decided instead to see a psychotherapist whom a friend had highly recommended. Ruth was a transpersonal therapist, working experientially with trauma, childhood conditioning, and past lives and guiding her clients in using their Higher Selves to help them in their self-explorations. She also did career therapy and discovered right away that Jamal had chosen engineering as his profession because his father and older brother were engineers and encouraged him to follow in their footsteps. He had never seriously considered doing anything else, and even though he liked his job, when he examined his deeper feelings, he discovered a strong sense of boredom and a longing to do something more creative.

Exploring the issue further revealed that his real love was science and doing research. This meant going back to school and getting a PhD in science. When he thought about doing that, he felt a lot of joy in his heart as well as a lot of anxiety. He had the money to quit his job and go to school, but he had planned to use the money to buy a house when he married Ayanna. She also wanted to start a family soon, which his going back to school would make impossible.

But the thought of not pursuing this new vocation now made Jamal feel sick again. When he told Ayanna, she was upset, too, as they had made the perfect plans for their future together.

His therapist helped him realize that the change could be made gradually. He needed to do some science courses to get a bachelor's degree in science, and he could do that online. Ayanna was thirty-two; perhaps she could wait a couple more years before starting a family.

They both would need to make some sacrifices, but doing the work Jamal was meant to do would make them both happier. If he continued being an engineer, he would become more disillusioned with life and that would make both their lives miserable.

Fortunately, Ayanna loved Jamal and was willing to help him. It would mean changing a lot of plans, but having him happy and not depressed was important to her. When he started his courses online, he felt like a different person. His moods ended, and he went on to get his PhD degree and ended up doing cancer research for a major company.

There are other areas in life that also can cause a person to come to a crossroad. Below is a list of some of these:

1. Needing to change careers.
2. Needing to change your job.
3. Looking at who you are in terms of your goals.
4. Being realistic about money and savings.
5. Needing to move to another apartment or house.

6. Wanting to change the location of where you live and work, but not knowing where to go.

7. Feeling trapped in a relationship.

8. Wanting to get married but not having met the right person yet and not knowing how to change that.

9. Feeling you want more than you can have, but not wanting to give up your desires.

10. Seeing the world around you changing and feeling that you can't change with it.

11. Not being able to help the people you love if they need your help.

12. Having inner desires that aren't realistic.

13. Wanting to change the way you look, but when you try, it never works out.

14. Having a hard time deciding who you can trust with private information.

15. Looking at life through shades of grey.

16. Deciding when to follow through with something and when not to.

17. Not trusting yourself to make the right decision.

18. When you think about your past decisions, feeling that you made the wrong ones and it's too late to change them.

19. Seeing life always as too difficult and too challenging.

Exercise One:

*Look at the above list and take one item at a time, and rate yourself from one to ten, ten being the highest rating in terms of the statement. If the statement has no meaning in your life at this time, just rate it a zero.*

*Take the statements that are rated five to ten and chose the ones you want to change. Take the one that is most important to you and ask your Higher Self the following questions. If the Higher Self doesn't agree with your rating, ask:*

1. *Is this something that I can change at this time?*
   - *If the answer is no, ask: Why not?*
     - *Take that answer and ask: Is there any way I can change this?*
     - *If the answer is no, ask: In the future will I be able to change this?*
       - *If the answer is no, ask: Why not?*
2. *If you believe in past lives, ask: Is this dilemma something I felt in a past life?*
   - *If the answer is yes, ask: Can you tell me more about it?*

Sometimes a crossroads has to do with your spiritual practice. If you are studying a specific teaching, there may be things in it that you have difficulty deciding about. Some of them can be the following:

1. You are new in a teaching and cannot decide if it is the right teaching for you.
2. Some of the people you know in the teaching make you question if they are meant to be your brothers and sisters.
3. When you attend a class you sometimes feel you don't belong.
4. You really like one aspect of the teaching, but another aspect doesn't interest you.
5. You aren't certain who would be the best person in the teaching to be your coach.

6.  You don't know if you really like to meditate.

7.  If you are working with the Higher Self, you often don't feel connected and don't know how to change that.

8.  Sometimes you question what you read but aren't sure about saying anything to anyone about it.

9.  Looking at your spiritual beliefs, you feel you don't know very much about the spiritual path.

10. You sometimes think it's good to take a rest from the teaching but don't know what is making you feel that way.

*Exercise Two:*

*Look at the above list and take one item at a time and rate yourself from one to ten, ten being the highest. If the statement has no meaning in your life at this time, just rate it a zero.*

*Take the statements that are rated five to ten and chose the ones you want to change. Take the one that is most important to you and ask your Higher Self the following questions. If the Higher Self doesn't agree with your rating, ask:*

1.  *Is this something that I can change at this time?*
    - *If the answer is no, ask: Why not?*
        - *Take that answer and ask: Is there any way I can change this?*
            - *If the answer is no, ask: In the future will I be able to change this?*
    - *If the answer is yes, you can change this situation at this time, ask: How can I change this? Please give me a process and a first step.*

2.  *If you believe in past lives, ask: Is this dilemma*

*something I felt in a past life when I was in a spiritual teaching?*
- *If the answer is yes, ask: Can you tell me more about it?*

Entering any kind of crossroads can sometimes make you get stuck and leave you feeling helpless as to what to do. If this happens to you now or in the future, it's best to rest, take time to distance yourself from the situation, and only when you feel clearer in your thinking do the following:

*Exercise Three:*
*Close your eyes, look at the crossroads, and think about what would be a good solution to it would be.*

*Then take whatever you came up with, put it in your heart, and ask your heart if this is a good solution.*

*Take that answer back to your mind and think about it again.*

*Again, put those thoughts back in your heart, and ask your heart if this is a good solution.*

*Keep doing this process until you feel that what you have in the end is what would work best.*

*Put that solution away for a couple of days, then meditate and ask your Higher Self the following questions:*
1. *Is my solution to this situation correct?*
   - *If the answer is no, ask: Why not?*
     - *Take that answer and ask: Is there any way I can change this?*
     - *If the answer is no, ask: In the future, will I want to change this?*
   - *If the answer is yes, you can change this situation at this time, ask: How can I change this? Please*

*give me a process and a first step.*

2. *If you believe in past lives, ask: Is this dilemma something I felt in a past life when I was in a spiritual teaching?*

   • *If the answer is yes, ask: Can you tell me more about it?*

Crossroads not only occur frequently in your own life, but they also occur with people you are close to. When it happens that you and someone else need to face the same crossroads, it is best to do the above exercise separately and then compare notes. Try to come to a final solution that takes in both of your results.

Remember to be open to change. Sometimes crossroads happen because you resist making a change in your life that is important for you to do. Don't be afraid to move forward. Also never fear that change will end up wrong and negative. There are always ways and times to change again. Life is an adventure, one that is never static but open for you to climb and grow.

# Time is Looked at Differently by a Yogi

What I mean by the Chapter Ten title is that a yogi judges time in a way that is not in keeping with how most people look at it. In most of the world, time is counted in terms of hours and days etc. For example, if you order a product from a supplier of some kind, prompt delivery by a certain date is often a measure of success. Or you need to finish a project in a certain amount of time with a set finish date. If you don't achieve the goal on time, you may be penalized. Even if you are given extra time, the fact that you didn't meet the first deadline will be noted and judged.

Yogis, on the other hand, see time more as representing periods of transition from one state to another. If a yogi is given a spiritual project to do with a goal in mind, the time may vary completely according to the person who is given the project. One yogi may be able to achieve that goal more quickly than another yogi, but the yogi who takes longer will never be penalized and will have no judgments made because she took longer.

Yogis in general are not bound by the limits of physical time when doing spiritual work. The only thing they are bound by is achieving the goal given to them. Even if they fail to complete the project, there will not be the same condemnation there would be of a non-yogi. But if a yogi does fail, the same project will be given to another yogi to try to complete. Many a yogi has been assigned a project and has not followed through with it, so the project is then given to someone else. In the yoga system there are always people lined up to do a project in case the original person fails to do it. This is why important plans that relate to evolution are always assigned to someone who the teachers know will follow through and that there is always a backup person just in case something happens to prevent the first person from completing the task. The following story is about this:

Juan was new to a yoga teaching, but even though he was new he was completely committed to his teacher and to the teaching itself. When he first started going to classes, he felt that he not only belonged but that he was following his true destiny. It felt right to him.

After a year in the group, his teacher asked to meet with him privately. In the meeting, Juan was asked to be in charge of a program the teacher was starting that consisted of bringing together people in the community to develop and build educational resources for underprivileged children.

Juan had a background in education and was a schoolteacher, but he had no knowledge of how to bring in outside sources, develop a volunteer program, or find funding for such a program. He questioned his teacher about selecting him for the job, which seemed overwhelming to him when he read the program's requirements. He also was married and worked full time. Juan's teacher also told him it was a project that he wanted to get off the ground and operating in a year's time. He said that Juan was chosen because he had the ability to take on such a program and complete it.

Not being able to say no to his teacher, John went home and meditated and asked for help to even begin such a huge enterprise. Determined to do the work, he adjusted his schedule, looked at all the areas where he would need advice and help and started talking to people in his circle of friends, to join him. It was a slow start because he had to determine exactly what to do first and how to do it. Honestly, he felt a year wasn't enough time and decided to not even think about that as a deadline. He first wrote up the program and what its goals were. Then he slowly made the right connections, found people who volunteered to help, and even got some support from local funding organizations.

Every six weeks John would send a report of his progress to his teacher. Once in a while, his teacher would make a suggestion but rarely said very much. This bothered Juan, as he was uncertain whether his teacher approved of his work. When he asked his teacher how he was doing, his teacher's response was a big smile, which pleased John but didn't make him feel everything was going correctly.

Underprivileged children were coming to the programs and the results started to bode well when there was a sudden mishap. One of the children claimed he was abused by one of the volunteer trainers. This caused a lot of havoc in the group, especially when there was a write-up about it in the local news. It made the program take some downfalls, and that caused Juan to feel he was failing. On top of that, his marriage was going through some difficulties. His wife was tired of his long hours doing the work and spending very little time with her and their child. Juan had been trying to be more attentive when the allegation of abuse occurred, which really was an upset for the organization.

The deadline Juan's teacher had given him was almost up and he wasn't halfway through what had been expected of him. Juan went to his teacher and apologized, and said he had felt he wasn't the right person, and now he was certain that was true. Someone else would have done a better job, and it would be all right if his teacher assigned someone else to take over the program.

His teacher said no, he still felt Juan could do it, and made some helpful suggestions. He also told him that he needed to take a break, that he was overdoing it, and needed to go away for a few days with his family.

This surprised Juan and he said, "But you wanted this to be done in a year. How can I do that?"

"A year would have been nice," his teacher replied, "but it's better to take longer and be a leader who is doing a good job and enjoying it. You have been overworking and so have lost your enthusiasm and joy of accomplishment. If it takes longer, that's fine. It's better for all of you to feel fulfilled in doing work that will help these poor children. Never make any work a hardship, and certainly never hurt the ones you love in doing this project."

"So, I haven't failed because it is taking so much longer?"

"No, I felt that you were the best person to do this job, and I was right. Do this work with joy in your heart, for the work itself, not just because I asked you to do it."

John took his teacher's advice, went on vacation with his family and rescheduled his time and the program. When it started to get a lot of funding, he quit his job and became the Executive Director full time. It was a job he loved doing.

Sometimes a person will see herself as having a lot of things to accomplish, and because it is a long list, it can cause her to feel it's too much—she isn't doing the work she was meant to do to develop as a yogi. A true yoga teaching does not believe in fanaticism, and when someone feels she has to be perfect and do more than it is possible, then that starts to spur fanaticism.

Look at how you allocate your time. Do you do it in a way that most people do, or do you do it as a yogi? You may have to do something in your house, and you schedule time to accomplish this. Then, suddenly something comes up that requires you to help someone else, and you feel that is more important. You often postpone your project to help others. As a result, it makes you feel you are a better yogi.

In actuality, that may not be true. Even a yogi has to look at time in a way that is right for her. Giving to others is part of the yoga tradition; but it is also important to give to yourself, or you will become a workaholic.

Juan's teacher gave him only a year to develop this big program. He did this on purpose because he knew that Juan would become the yogi workaholic. He wanted him to know that it's okay to say no—that it was too short a time to do such a program and work full time. Because Juan couldn't do it in the requested time ,he felt he was a failure. This was a good learning for him to realize how he felt about himself and his skills. Juan also was viewing this project as a sacrifice in his life, instead of realizing that it was starting his true work and his destined vocation. He was meant to be a leader, and this work made him develop and become one.

Time for a yogi has to relate to her destiny, whether in her vocation, in her spiritual practice, or in her relationships with others. Overdoing one area lacks balance. This teaching promotes balance in life. Only balance can give a yogi the way to grow spiritually.

*Exercise One:*

*Make a list of the things you do daily in a week's time during your waking hours. If you have a full-time job, also include the things you do on your days off. The list should include any spiritual practice, exercise, and mundane tasks such as shopping, cleaning, etc. Also add time you spend doing enjoyable things that relate to your social life.*

*You needn't structure this list into a schedule; instead, mainly* come up with a general understanding of how you spend your time.

Then take whatever you came up with, put it in your heart, and ask your heart if this is a good solution.

Now take the list and underline all the things that you positively need to do in that week with a black line. Obviously, if you have a full-time job, those hours will be underlined. If you always meditate every day, that would be underlined. Make sure you underline something that you know you can't give up and that is important for you to do, even if it's something very mundane, like doing your laundry.

Those underlined items should only be a part of the list. If you find that they comprise more than two-thirds of it, then you need to reexamine what you have written. To help you in the process, you will add another line in color under the black ones:

If something is the most important and you know it has to be done, such as going to a job, add a red line under the black one.

For something you feel comes next in importance, add a green line under the black.

Then there will be those things you feel should do but you are more flexible about. Make this a blue line under the black line.

If originally your list had black lines for more than two thirds of the list, you can now remove the black lines from some of the green- and blue-lined items until the things you feel obligated to do. Do not exceed two-thirds of the total. The items you took off can be added to those things on your list that had no underlines. These are the things that you want and like to do but sometimes don't have the time to do.

Even if your lined list was two-thirds or less, still look it over carefully to be sure you want to do everything on the list.

This exercise gives you a better understanding of how you allocate your time. It should give you flexibility to know what is important for you still to do and what can be done in your one-third free time. Make sure that those items are things that will be fun and bring beauty into your life. They could include nature walks, museum visits, and entertainment of any kind that you enjoy.

A yogi also has the ability to adjust her schedule to include the spiritual aspects of her teaching. Meditation is considered very important, but sometimes a student loses the rhythm of meditating every day by taking time out, so that when she returns she has to build up the rhythm once more. Usually, a student feels the change and tries harder to keep the rhythm in the future. It's important to do this; but it's more important to honor your feelings, particularly if you are going through a period that causes you to stop your practice because of outside things occurring.

A teacher should never be harsh with a student who is going through problems that need to be taken care of; and a student should never feel guilty and anxious if she has to attend to other things, rather than her daily practice. This teaching believes in discipline, but not to the extreme where it interferes with daily life.

Someone entering a spiritual teaching may strive to advance and then confront an obstacle that keeps her from continuing in the same manner. Challenges will always happen and when they occur, realize that everything you go through helps you spiritually, even when it seems mainly a burden you have to overcome. Life always brings challenges. When that happens see them as a way of learning. Without them, life will be static and often boring. Some challenges bring you hardship and others bring you joy. Going through them always gives you a deeper understanding of yourself and others. Welcome them. Know they are happening to reveal an important lesson you need to learn.

*Exercise Two:*

*Think of a challenge you had to face in the past year or two and ask your Higher Self the following questions:*

1. *Was this something I needed to go through?*
   - *If the answer is yes, ask: Why?*
   - *If the answer is no, I didn't need to go through this, ask: Could I have avoided it happening?*
     - *If the answer is yes, ask: What should I have done?*
     - *Did I handle this challenge correctly?*
   - *If the answer is no, ask: What should I have done instead?*

2. *Was there something I needed to learn from it?*
   - *If the answer is yes, ask: What was it?*
   - *If the answer is no, I didn't need to go through this, ask: Could I have avoided it happening?*
     - *If the answer is yes, ask: What should I have done?*
     - *If the answer is no, ask: What should I have done instead?*
     - *Did I handle this challenge correctly?*

Challenges and obstacles can also take away your time, making the list you made earlier in the chapter impossible to keep. They usually take over all the time available and leave a person enervated with a feeling of failure. This also is part of a yogi's path. See them as lessons that help you to continue. Look at them as the detours that take time to handle but never permanently stop your journey. If the same challenge occurs several times, realize you haven't learned the lesson. The next time the challenge occurs, learn with clearer eyes and heart and understand what it wants to teach you.

As I have stated before, it doesn't matter how long it takes to resolve a challenge or obstacle; what matters is that you come through it, learn the lesson, and continue onward.

### Chapter Eleven
# Looking at Your Mission in Life

When this teaching talks about mission, it doesn't mean dharma, which is much more than someone's mission. Dharma covers many areas in a person's life. Mission also doesn't mean a person's vocation, which is part of dharma. Mission relates more to the spiritual part of dharma. If you were meant to do a specific type of work that is related to your spiritual growth that would be a mission.

Your teacher asks you to join one of the committees in the teaching. An example would be joining the Retreat Committee, which is in charge of the operation and material of the retreats, or the teacher may ask you to be on the board of either Higher Self Yoga or the Culture Shift Collaborative (formerly the Center for Peace through Culture). Also, on the Higher Self Yoga website, there are different groups that are run by the disciples in this organization.

Missions of any kind can be small or large depending on the person. Many things that need to be done to keep any organization functioning can be called a mission. It is what is called being of service. Sometimes a teacher or Mahatma or Tara will ask a student to do a particular mission, and other times the student himself volunteers to help in some capacity. Usually mission work is never paid, unless it is a professional job that requires a person to devote many hours of work. Generally, all the missions in the esoteric part of Higher Self Yoga are never paid. Also the people on the board in both organizations are never paid for those positions.

Missions usually are voluntary except for the few times when the teacher or Mahatma or Tara asks a student to do a particular task. Even then, if the student is too busy in their mundane lives to do the work, it is fine for a student to decline at that time but be open to helping when he is not too overly occupied. When a student is asked to do something, it is important to meditate on it, and ask the Higher Self if it is the right mission for him to do at that time.

This is particularly important if another student asks for help in something he is doing that relates to the teaching. If someone helps a spiritual brother or sister, that is not considered a mission, but an act of good will and kindness.

This teaching also has a component of doing service in the world. Sometimes that service relates to the teaching, which is a mission connected to one of the two organizations mentioned above. Other times, service includes helping in other capacities, such as volunteering to help other organizations that are doing good work in the community. This could mean visiting veterans or patients in a hospital or working in groups that help the needy. There are many worthwhile organizations that need volunteers.

The reason why doing a mission, or doing service of some kind, is so important is because it focuses on developing skills that don't necessarily relate to a person's vocation. For example, a doctor or a scientist may be on a corporate board and have to learn how to work with a group of people from different walks of life. A person, who works in an office may volunteer to work with handicapped children and learn compassion. Doing service is what in the yoga tradition is referred to as Karma Yoga.

Mainly, a mission is important for spiritual growth. It helps a person learn things about himself that doing his regular work doesn't necessarily teach. If it is working with spiritual brothers and sisters, it can also enhance relationships and create a bond with others that a person may never have felt was possible. Of course, it can also do the opposite and cause competition and negative feelings to arise, which is also part of the spiritual journey. Too often someone avoids a brother or sister because of past life relationships, but having to work with each other cannot only uncover the past, it can help heal it. It's all a learning process. The following story illustrates this.

Maria joined a yoga teaching and found her teacher when a friend of hers, Estella, introduced her to the teaching. She immediately joined Estella's class and started attending the weekly sessions.

There was a man in the class, Juan, that Maria instantly disliked, and when she mentioned her feelings to Estella, Estella told her that Juan was really a lovely person— maybe Maria had a negative past life with him that was causing her reaction. She also advised Maria to talk to him and try to discover what their past had been. Following her friend's advice, Maria met with Juan. When they meditated together, he saw that she had been his wife in the eighteenth century, and he had run away with another woman, leaving her and their children destitute. It had been a difficult life for Maria.

Knowing this was helpful for Maria, but she couldn't get over her feelings of dislike toward Juan. He himself also felt a deep sense of remorse and tried to avoid her at any class functions. They simply could never be friends and both of them knew it.

Once a year, their teacher led a week's retreat that all of his students would attend. During the retreat, the teacher formed a committee to be in charge of setting up programs around the country that would carry the teaching to places where there were no classes. These programs would be featured on their website as a way of attracting more people to the teaching. Several people on the committee would introduce the teacher when he conducted sessions. Some of the more advanced disciples would also participate in this outreach.

The committee was comprised of ten people and two of them were Maria and Juan. Both privately spoke to their teacher and told him that it would be difficult for them to work together because of their past history. He simply smiled and said, "The past is the past, now is the now. Let go of the past and stay in the present." They said they would try to do that.

At first, it was very difficult—they both were silent and didn't contribute much to the discussion. The leader of the committee, Marco, spoke to the teacher about it, who explained, "Give it time. They have to become more comfortable with each other before they can contribute."

The teacher also explained he hoped they would get over their past feelings. They both were excellent workers, and he had chosen them because of their understanding and expertise in this field. Maria was in charge of social media for her company, and Juan was a program director for his firm. The teacher clarified that normally he wouldn't put two people on a committee who had negative past history, but because of their skills he thought he would give it a try.

Interestingly, the two of them were single, in their thirties and very attractive. Underneath the dislike and remorse was an attraction they both felt. As the plans started to formulate, they became involved and found that they could work well together. Soon they were the main people developing the programming. Maria realized that Estella's assessment of Juan was correct.

He was a very warm-hearted and nice person. Juan also began to let go of his guilt feelings about Maria and recognized her qualities and enjoyed working with her. Even though there was an attraction, they both realized that they needed to keep their relationship just a friendship; anything more than that could very well pull them back into the past.

Sometimes, when you are in a spiritual teaching, you aren't given a mission to do. Usually this is because of one or more of the following reasons:

1. Your mission hasn't been decided yet by your teacher or Mahatma or Tara. This could be for several reasons. It may depend on your spiritual progress, or it could also depend on your psychological problems that need to be healed.

2. Your mission depends on outside factors that have to be put in place first.

3. Your mission may have several parts that need to prepare you to do it.

4. Your mission could be composed of a series of missions that branch out and the direction hasn't yet been determined.

5. Your mission involves other people who haven't come on board yet, and by the time they do, the mission may change and be one you are no longer part of.

6. Your mission requires a lot to time to fulfill, and currently you wouldn't have the time to pursue it.

7. Your mission hasn't been formulated yet because it depends on what is happening on the planet.

8. You may have a mission that was given to you before you were born, and the course of your life has taken you off track. You first need to go back to the original

concept.

9. You may be in line to take over someone else's mission if the person doesn't follow through and accomplish it.

10. Your mission will take you in directions that you aren't ready to do yet.

*Exercise One:*

*If you are in a spiritual teaching, but haven't chosen a teacher yet, ask your Higher Self the following questions:*

1. *Can you tell me what my mission is?*
   - *If the answer is yes, ask: What is it?*
   - *If the answer is no, ask: Why not?*
     - *If the answer is that you are not ready to know it, go through the above twenty reasons, and ask your Higher Self whether each one is the reason.*
2. *If the Higher Self answered no about all of the above, ask: Can you tell me what the reason it?*
   - *Take that answer and discuss it more with your Higher Self.*

Basically, everyone in a spiritual teaching has a mission, whether it is a small one or a large one. Missions can change, so maybe what you believe your mission is will be changed as you develop spiritually. Your Mahatma or Tara is the person who will make those changes, and sometimes the Mahatma or Tara doesn't tell your teacher what your mission is.

There are various reasons for this. For instance, if it is a very important mission, the person needs to grow spiritually and that may not happen, and the mission will have to be given to someone else. It's therefore best that the teacher or the student doesn't know what the mission is. It can be disappointing to the teacher and the student if the student fails.

If you have a teacher, it is best to ask the teacher what your mission is. But realize what your mission is now can change and even change radically.

Disciples are always tested, and in part those tests also determine whether someone is ready for a specific mission.

Doing service of any kind, on the other hand, is something you can determine for yourself.

*Exercise Two:*

*Make a list of all the things you feel you would like to do that are service-oriented. They can be things in the teaching or in your outside life that interest you, or even both.*

*After you have completed your list, take each item and ask your Higher Self the following questions:*

*Is this something I would enjoy doing?*

- *If the answer is no, ask: Why not?*

*When you have gone through the list and have eliminated the ones that the Higher Self said no to, take the remaining items, put each one in your heart, and ask yourself if this is the service you should do at this time.*

- *If your heart responds yes, write that item down on a separate sheet of paper.*

*If you have more than one item on the new sheet, take each one and ask your Higher Self:*

*Is this the one I should do at this time?*

- *If the answer is no, ask: Why not?*

*Maybe you will end up with more than one thing to do, which would be fine. If you feel it is too much to do at this time, again*

*put each one in your heart and ask:*
- *Is this the one I should do at this time? Follow the response in your heart.*

Doing service or a mission will help you spiritually. Know that it can also bring you feelings of joy and accomplishment.

It is following your path and knowing that through service of any kind you will learn those things that you are meant to learn, and in so doing, it will help you progress spiritually.

*Exercise Three:*

*Write down the names of all the people you are very close to. They could be family, friends, or business partners. When you have completed that list, take each name and ask your Higher Self the following questions:*

1. *Is this someone I can talk to about the teaching?*
   - *If the answer is no, ask: Why not?*
2. *Take that answer and ask: Will this change in the future?*
   - *If the answer is yes, ask: When will that be possible?*
   - *If the answer is no, it will not change in the future, ask: Will this eventually affect our relationship?*
     - *If the answer is yes, ask: What will happen?*
     - *If the answer is no, ask: If the subject comes up, how do I handle it?*

Besides dealing with others in terms of talking about your teaching, the other problem that can arise has to do with the time you spend studying and practicing it. Since you may have previously spent your time with those people, when you begin to cut back on that it can cause friction, especially if the person is someone you live with or spend time with. Obviously, those people will need to know what you are doing. If you previously spent a lot of time with someone, you would have to explain that you can't do as much now. This can cause jealousy to occur. It's important then to talk to the person explaining how much the teaching means to you, and also bring in how much you honor and enjoy your friendship. If the person still feels slighted, listen to her, and try to come up with a solution that would work for both of you.

*Exercise Three:*
*Write down the names of all the people you are very close to. It can be family, friends, or business partners. When you have completed that list, take each name and ask your Higher Self the following questions:*

1. *If this someone I can talk to about the teaching?*
2. *If the answer is no, ask: Why not?*
3. *Take that answer and ask: Will this change in the future?*
4. *If the answer is yes, ask: When will that be possible?*
5. *If the answer is no, it will not change in the future, ask: Will this eventually affect our relationship?*
   - *If the answer is yes, ask: What will happen?*
   - *If the answer is no, ask: If the subject comes up, how do I handle it?*

### Chapter Twelve

# Being Aware of Others in Terms of Your Spiritual Practice

Once you are in a spiritual practice you will usually tell the people in your life about the teaching. These are people with whom you are close to, and with whom you are in constant contact with. They could include a loved one, a business partner, or even a very close friend whom you see on a regular basis.

Often, you might have a difficult time explaining what the teaching is about, particularly to people who have no religious faith. Frequently, such a person will try to talk you out of continuing, especially if the person is a husband or a wife.

Sometimes, rather than cause a schism in the family, a student will decide not to continue, even though the teaching means a great deal to her. Unfortunately, leaving the teaching and even leaving the teacher can cause the student never to be completely happy again in the personal relationship that forced her to leave.

The same can happen with a close friendship, when the student's friend berates her for being in a spiritual teaching, and tries to convince her that she could be entering a cult. When this happens, it can make a student start to question if this teaching could be a cult. Even when the student looks more closely at the teaching and realizes that it doesn't have any of the qualities of cult behavior, she can still be wary of what she is entering. Others' criticism can cause doubt to come into a student's mind. It can also cause the student to break up the friendship, even a close and long one.

In a family situation, one can't just leave; so there may have to be a discussion that explains to a family member that being in this teaching is what you plan to do. You may have to explain that in the future you will no longer discuss the teaching with that person. Also, you may have to ask the person to honor your decisions and stop trying to change your mind about something you are strongly committed to. The following story illustrates this situation:

Erik was twenty-three when he discovered Higher Self Yoga and decided to study the esoteric part of the teaching. He lived in a major city where there was a class quite close to where he lived with two other roommates. They all had attended the same college and were roommates then, and after they graduated continued to live together. Two of them, Jay and Alan, had taken jobs in corporations, but Erik had decided to continue his schooling and was going for a master's degree in psychology. His goal was to be a child psychotherapist and maybe obtain a Ph.D. in the same field.

After attending the Higher Self Yoga class for a month and meeting his teacher, Jane, who came to one of the classes, Erik decided he would tell his roommates about the teaching. They were both surprised because the three of them had never discussed religion during all the years they lived together.

Jay thought it was interesting and even asked Erik some questions about it. Alan had the opposite reaction. He had been brought up in a strict Catholic family and even went to church once in a while. Immediately, he started questioning Erik about the teacher, what they did in class, what was the doctrine, all in a tone of voice that was very authoritarian and harsh.

This immediately made Erik defensive, and he refused to answer Alan's questions. This caused Alan to be even more adamant about wanting to know more of the details. Jay stepped in to try to stop what was becoming a loud and nasty argument.

Erik ended up leaving the apartment—just walking and walking to become calm again. He found that he was near his teacher's home and decided to see if she was in. Fortunately, she was, and she invited him in for a cup of coffee. Jane was a woman in her late forties, single, smart, with an inner sense of clarity. Erik by then was calm but was still feeling very disturbed by the argument he had just had. Jane saw something was wrong and asked him if she could be of help. Explaining what had happened to him, Erik told her he was at a loss as to what to do. Could she help him?

Jane thought about it for a few minutes and said, "Erik, the best thing to do is let it go. Alan sounds like he would never accept your becoming a yogi. You've been friends a long time. It's best to explain to him that you love him, that you have differences that obviously can't be reconciled, and that it would be best to longer talk about the teaching."

"Knowing him, I don't think he will be able to let it go like that. How should I handle it if he brings it up again?"

"Change the subject and if he persists, then leave the room, or go out."

Erik tried to follow this advice, but even though he calmly asked Alan to stop, Alan still brought the subject up—telling Erik he was concerned he had joined a cult. Erik knew in his heart that this wasn't true. When he talked to Jane again, she said if Alan didn't stop, then maybe Erik needed to consider getting a different place to live.

This made it difficult for Erik as he was on a limited income and couldn't afford a place of his own. He talked to Jay, and Jay agreed that he also was becoming tired of Alan's badgering. They both talked to Alan and told him that if he couldn't stop making nasty remarks about Erik's spiritual path they would leave and find another place to live without him. This really upset Alan, and when he looked at the way he had been behaving, he realized his fanaticism came from his Catholic upbringing and was causing his behavior. He apologized and finally stopped talking about Erik's teaching.

The three continued living together and went back to their good relationship with each other.

Some of you have been in the teaching for a while, so maybe this type of situation has happened to you already, or maybe you still need to talk to your friends and loved ones about being part of this group. If you are the latter, do the following exercise:

*Exercise One:*

> *Write down the names of all the people you are very close to. It can be family, friends, or business partners. When you have completed that list, take each name and ask your Higher Self the following questions:*
>
> 1. *Is this someone I can talk to about the teaching?*
>    - *If the answer is no, ask: Why not?*
> 2. *Take that answer and ask: Will this change in the future?*
> 3. *If the answer is yes, ask: When will that be possible?*
> 4. *If the answer is no, it will not change in the future, ask: Will this eventually affect our relationship?*
>    - *If the answer is yes, ask: What will happen?*
>    - *If the answer is yes, ask: What will happen?*

Besides dealing with others in terms of talking about your teaching, the other problem that can arise has to do with the time you spend studying and practicing it. Since you may have previous spent your time with those people, when you begin to cut back on that it can cause friction, especially if the person is someone you live with or spend time with. Obviously, those people will need to know what you are doing. If you previously spent a lot of time with someone, you will have to explain that you can't do as much now. This can cause jealousy. It's important then to talk to the person explaining how much the teaching means to you, also bring in how much you honor and enjoy your friendship. If the person still feels slighted, listen to her, and try to come up with a solution that would work for both of you.

*Exercise Two:*

> *Take the previous list of people you are close to and take out of the list those people you spend a lot of time with. Check to see if any of them are the ones your Higher Self has indicated you couldn't share the teaching with. Put these people on a separate list. Now take the ones you can talk to and taking each name ask the Higher Self the following questions:*
> 1. *Would this person understand why I might be spending less time with her?*
>    - *If the answer is no, ask: How can I explain it in a way that she would accept this?*
> 2. *Then ask: If she won't accept the reason, what do I need to do to make her be more understanding?*
> 3. *Also ask: Is it possible that we can come to a compromise that she can accept.*

After you have gone through each name, take the list of people you can't speak to about the teaching. These will be more difficult to deal with. This time when you ask your Higher Self about how to deal with the person explain in detail what the relationship is to your Higher Self. It may be a situation that you cannot change; otherwise, it would be too hurtful to the person.

For example, if you have a parent you see on a regular basis, you may not be able to cut that time down as the parent would feel hurt and rejected. Use your heart when it comes to the people on this list to determine if you have to make this person an exception in cutting back time with her. Realize that you may have to make a general excuse if the person asks why you aren't seeing her as much. Try not to lie, simply say you've been busy or have too much work.

*Exercise Three:*

*Take each name on this list, connect with your Higher Self and first explain about the relationship and then ask the Higher Self the following questions:*

1. *Is this someone I can cut back time with and she won't feel hurt?*
   - *If the Higher Self says no, ask: Is this someone for whom I have to make an exception?*
2. *If the answer is no, ask: How should I handle this situation, so the person doesn't feel hurt?*
3. *Also ask: If the person still is upset about it, and the person isn't an exception, what can I do to make this all right?*

Sometimes, you may have to say you are studying something and not go into any details. Make it sound like you would like to see more of the person but at this time it would be difficult. Also try to make up time now and then especially if you haven't seen the person for a while. Balancing friendships and love ones needs to be done by always asking your Higher Self for help. Be alert if you feel the person is feeling hurt that you aren't spending as much time together.

Fortunately, most people, if they love you, will understand that what you are doing is something that is very important to you, and they will accept it and not take it personally. Obviously, if you are married, your wife and your children should be exceptions. Only when you attend classes or retreats will you be taking time away from them. Quality time is also important. If you are with them and doing other things, then that is not quality time when you are sharing things with them. Always keep those you love in your heart, and when you are with them, be with them one hundred percent.

One last area that you need to consider when you start a spiritual practice is the kind of work you are doing. If you are in a job that requires a lot of your time, you will have to adjust your spiritual practice accordingly. Sometimes this cannot be avoided; but other times you may need to look at whether the extra hours you are putting into your job are really necessary. If you are always overworked, then maybe you need to speak to your supervisor and explain you need help. Or you may be doing a project that needs to be reassessed as to whether some of the work can be eliminated and isn't necessary. Often, a person follows a routine that can be shortened.

If none of this is possible, really examine if the job is one you want to do for the rest of your life, or could you find a comparable job that isn't so time consuming. Even if you don't have a spiritual practice, if you are overworked you may want to look for a better job that isn't so demanding. It's always important to have free time to enjoy life and develop relationships.

It's also important to love your job and the work you are doing. If you are bored, or unhappy with the work or the people you have to work with, then you need to seek a job where you can feel fulfilled and happy. Otherwise, any spiritual practice will be affected by those negative feelings. A spiritual practice can't change those feelings that come from unfulfilled work-related issues.

*Exercise Four:*

*Ask your Higher Self the following questions:*

1. *Is the work I am doing professionally giving me a feeling of fulfillment?*
   - *If the answer is no, ask: What is lacking?*
2. *Take that answer and examine it and ask: Can I bring this more into my work, or do I need to find another job where I would have this?*
3. *If the answer is yes, your job is fulfilling ask: Is there more that I should be doing that I'm not aware of?*
   - *If the answer is yes, ask: What is it?*

*Also look at the hours you are working and if they are more than an average job, ask your Higher Self the following questions:*

1. *Is there something I am doing that is causing me to work more hours than I should?*
   - *If the answer is yes, ask: What do I need to change?*
2. *If the answer is no, ask: Can I address this to my superiors?*
   - *If the answer is no, ask: What would be the best solution to this problem?*

Your professional life, your personal life, and your spiritual life should bring you fulfillment and happiness. If any of them are making you feel tired, overworked, and unhappy, then you need to look at why you are feeling this way. It's important to have a life that is not only fulfilling but one that brings you contentment and happiness. Of course, there will always be challenges and difficulties that you have to face and go through, but you can do that easily if you ask for help from your Higher Self. If you have a teacher, know your teacher is always there to advise and help you on your spiritual journey.

### Chapter Thirteen

## Seeing the Road You Have Traveled with New Eyes

When you have been on the road for several years, it sometimes needs to be examined again. The road, also called the path, is the one you enter when you come into any spiritual teaching. Each person's journey will always differ from another's, but there are similarities that can help a person arriving at the same place where someone else has preceded him.

Usually, a person can learn more if he stops at each place and meditates about the best way in which to continue. The energy of the path that has had many previous travelers can be felt, and that energy will be a guide for the new person arriving there.

Often on the road you may reach an obstacle that causes you to turn back. When that happens, it's important not to feel you have failed. Realize that this is what happens to everyone on a spiritual journey. It's best to pause and again revisit the journey you have just taken, so that if you have to go back, you will know how to move forward through the obstacle when you encounter it again.

When you think about what you have already traveled through successfully, it's important to feel the vibration that you have created, and then let that positive vibration renew you when you are facing the obstacles.

The following is a list of some of the obstacles that many students encounter on the path:

1. Resistance that comes from feelings of unworthiness.
2. Not understanding your strengths and weaknesses.
3. Learning the teaching but not applying it in daily life.
4. Forgetting to ask for help from your Higher Self and your teacher.
5. Knowing you can do better but not trying.
6. Seeing yourself as inferior to others who are more advanced.
7. Believing you have achieved all that you are able to achieve.
8. Seeing yourself as someone who will always be stuck in one way or another.
9. Learning the right methods to keep moving forward but not noticing some of the markers that are there to help guide you.
10. Wanting to grow spiritually but never putting that desire into the heart.
11. Seeing yourself as a yogi but limiting that understanding to a few practices.
12. Believing you are doing well and being steadfast, yet always staying in one place for a long time and not understanding why.
13. Looking at your mundane life and feeling you can't change anything in it that is causing you difficulty or even heart ache.
14. Wanting to succeed but not having the discipline to do so.
15. Expecting your teacher to guide you all the way to the end, but not putting in the right effort that is your part in the journey.

The spiritual road is a symbol for a student to use. It has a beginning and an end.

The beginning is when you enter the teaching and decide to start your journey. The end is when you have achieved becoming a Mahatma (male) or a Tara (female), one who has achieved seven initiations. The road starts out wide and ends in a path that is very difficult to transverse. During the journey you encounter all the personal obstacles that relate to who you are. Some of these are listed above.

You also have to go through many spiritual tests that your teacher and Mahatma or Tara have specifically designed to help you understand what your need to work on spiritually. All the challenges that happen will help you overcome many of the psychological problems you have developed through all your lifetimes. These problems may be hidden in your present incarnation, but they will be reawakened during your journey, and in that reawakening they need to be healed or transmuted if they are negative. No matter where you are now on the path, it's important to review what you have done previously, and recognize if you have succeeded in overcoming those characteristics that are negative and have awakened those that are positive.

When you review the path that you have already tread, be aware that even if you have to turn back to confront something you didn't fully overcome before, that doing it now is much better than having it come up stronger down the way.

*Exercise One:*

*Look at the list of fifteen obstacles above and taking each one rate yourself from one to ten in terms of having faced this obstacle, making ten the highest rating. After you have done this, ask your Higher Self to rate you on the obstacle. .*

*If the Higher Self's rating differs from yours, ask the Higher Self the following questions:*

1.  *If the Higher Self's rating is higher, ask: Why did I rate myself lower?*
    -   *Also ask: What am I not seeing about myself?*
2.  *If the Higher Self's rating is lower, ask: Why did I rate myself higher?*
    -   *Also ask: What am I not seeing about myself?*

*Next, take the Higher Self's list of ratings and prioritize them, putting the highest-rated one on top. Taking the top one, ask the Higher Self the following questions:*

3.  *Is this an obstacle I developed in childhood?*
    -   *If the answer is yes, say, Please give me a process and a first step in healing this obstacle.*
    -   *If the answer is no, ask, When did I develop this obstacle?*
4.  *Take that answer and ask, Can I overcome this obstacle myself or do I need to have help?*
    -   *If the answer is yes, say, pease give me a process and a first step in healing this obstacle.*
    -   *If the answer is no, you need help, ask, Is it something for which I need to seek therapy, or is it something my teacher can help me with?*

*Do the above exercise with some of the other top obstacles on your list.*

*Now, working with one of these obstacles, look back on your journey so far. Notice when this obstacle came up, and if you noticed it and worked on it; or if it was something you might have noticed and tried to leave behind without working on it. If it was the latter, ask your Higher Self the following questions:*

5.  *Why didn't I work on this obstacle at the time?*

6. *Take that answer and ask, Is this something I will continue to do when I see this obstacle?*
   - *If the answer is yes, ask: How can I overcome this reaction and do the work I need to do to heal this?*
   - *If the answer is no, ask: Please give me a process and a first step in starting to overcome this.*

Even when you work on an obstacle and are able to heal it and continue on your journey, it may come up again later for you in another form, or even in a lesser form. This means it still needs to be watched and worked with. This is why you need to look back and evaluate your journey as you continue down the road. Seeing it with new eyes means seeing it from a place later on where you can notice those areas that still need work. The following story illustrates this point:

Mary was a disciple for seven years and had developed spiritually during that time. She was very much loved by her spiritual brothers and sisters and was considered someone who could go far in the teaching. Her relationship with her teacher was one of devotion and love. Her main psychological problems came from having been in a dysfunctional family where there was verbal abuse from her mother and indifference from her father. Her two brothers were favored by both her parents, who expected her to wait on them because she was the oldest and a girl.

As soon as Mary was eighteen, she left home and went to college, obtaining a scholarship and working part-time to cover her expenses. She ended up in corporate law and found a job in a large prestigious corporation.

Mary met her spiritual teacher when she was twenty-five and now, at thirty-two, she was living in a beautiful apartment and seriously dating another lawyer she had met during her career.

When she entered the teaching, her teacher told her she needed to do therapy—she had problems caused by her childhood conditioning that needed healing.

She was in therapy for several years working on her wounded inner child and her relationship with her parents and brothers. It was very deep work and helped her understand her feelings of unworthiness.

During Mary's therapy work she became a disciple. When an obstacle came up, she really looked at it, and with help from her therapist and teacher was able to overcome the obstacle and move forward.

She had achieved two initiations on the path when she encountered another obstacle that she had previously noticed in passing, but had never thought was very important. This time it became much larger and stopped her completely, as if someone had punched her in the stomach. It concerned her relationship with Pierre, her boyfriend.

They were thinking of living together and were starting to discuss the legalities etc. Mary thought it best if they rented an apartment together and kept their own condos, which they owned separately and were too small for two people. This way if the relationship didn't work out they could move back to their own condos. Pierre disagreed and felt hurt that she would in any way be negative about things not working out. Mary said she was just realistic; living together was different from just spending weekends together. It was more of a commitment.

She explained that often, when people moved in together, they ended up separating. Pierre in turn, said he wouldn't have suggested living together if he weren't committed to it working out with her. The more he insisted, the more Mary became adamant about what she felt and wanted. It ended up in their first major fight.

When Mary talked to her teacher about what had happened, he asked her, "In therapy did you talk about your relationships with your brothers? I think you said they were bossy and told you what to do."

"Yes, I worked on that, but they aren't anything like Pierre. He has never been bossy. This is the first time he ever raised his voice to me. But now I know I am right: things can go wrong when you live together."

Her teacher smiled. "Yes, that's true, things will always go wrong, but if you love each other, you can always work it out. It seems to me that you haven't really resolved your relationship with your brothers. Your fear is that Pierre is going to treat you the way they did, and you will have to leave him, like you left your family."

"You're right, I am afraid; that's why I want to keep my condo, just in case."

"I know you love Pierre, and he sounds very committed to being with you. Tell him that, and maybe do some more work with your therapist about your relationship with your brothers."

Mary talked to Pierre about her fears, and they decided to wait to live together until she could work more with her therapist. Six months later they did get a bigger place. Both sold their condos, and, after living together for two years, they decided to get married.

Sometimes a student will discover an obstacle that he has no knowledge about, as in Mary's story. The hidden obstacle is not necessarily related to the teaching.

An obstacle can also come from a past life and never appear until the student starts his spiritual journey. Usually when this happens the student can look at it honestly, and the work will seem easier since the student isn't acting it out in this life. But this isn't always true. For example, you may suddenly have feelings of resentment toward a fellow student whom you had been friendly with. These feelings can be ones you never experienced before, even when you were irritated or upset with someone. The feelings are so strong, they cause you to feel an anger you never knew you had.

You know it must be from a past life. Finding out about that life, you realize what the person did to you was awful and unforgivable. The feelings are so intense you can't explain them with any rationale. You don't want to express them to the person, whom in this life you like, but they are hurting you physically and mentally. The teacher can certainly help you and therapeutically you can work out the anger by going to a boxing club or pursuing any activity that will release the feelings.

When an unknown feeling comes up like that, it's very important not to disregard it. Find out the source, but realize it is part of you, even though you haven't acted on it in this lifetime. Once the feeling is there, it will be an obstacle that you have to keep your eye on.

The spiritual road will bring you many moments of heartbreak, discovery, and joy. It contains everything; and as it narrows into a path, realize you have traveled it for a long time, not only in this life but in many lives before. Some of the obstacles will be new this time, but when this life ends you will have seen many of the ones you have had to encounter other lifetimes.

### Chapter Fourteen

# Discovering New Ways to Do Your
# Spiritual Practice

This chapter will introduce you to the different ways in which you can bring the teaching into your life. Obviously, there are some things that are best to do to help you grow spiritually. Some of these are the following:

1. Having a daily routine of meditation
2. Attending class and doing the classwork beforehand
3. Looking at nature and connecting to the elementals
4. Having a routine in which you work with a buddy and share different exercises
5. Devoting time to following any service you have decided to do

These are the main things that every student should try to accomplish on a regular basis.

There are other things, though, that would be good to do that maybe you haven't thought about, things that are sometimes not related to the teaching but are actions that still help you grow spiritually. Some of these are the following:

1. Developing friendships with some of your brothers and sisters

2. Offering to help others when you hear someone is in need of assistance

3. Being part of a community and serving in a role that is helpful to others in your community

4. If you are one of the healers in the group, daily sending healing to those people on your healing list

5. Giving advice when someone needs help or assistance

6. Being a consultant for new people coming into the teaching

7. When there is an event or a retreat, offering to help

8. Always asking the teacher if she needs anything and volunteering to be of service to her

9. When the teacher asks for questions to be sent to her to be answered in class, always being aware when you read the books of things you would like to know more about

10. Knowing how to best explain the teaching to others in your life

11. Being committed to your own spiritual growth

12. If the teacher asks you to be part of a committee, to feel happy you have been selected to do that work

13. Learning discernment about the things that are happening to you in your life

14. Seeing that you are part of a community, and knowing you want to fulfill your role in it, and assist others in it who need help

15. Looking at your future with clarity of purpose

16. Staying centered and in your heart in your daily work and practice

17. When you finish every day, thanking those who have helped you

18. Developing your relationship with your Higher Self
19. Believing that no matter how difficult the obstacles can be, that you will overcome them
20. Making the teaching part of your life—not a separate part, but one that directs and guides you

You probably are doing many things on this list; and there are also things that wouldn't interest you, especially if your life is busy with outside activities you have to do. When you look at this second list, see if you can incorporate some of them in with your practice of the five things in the first list. For example, number five in the second list, "Giving advice when someone needs help or assistance," can be included in number three on the first list, "Looking at nature and connecting to the elementals." Maybe one of your brothers or sisters is having a difficult time linking with the elementals. You could walk with her in nature and show her the best way to connect with them. This activity would also incorporate number one on the second list, "Developing friendships with some of your brothers and sisters."

It's also good to shake up your routine regarding the first five items. For example, instead of meditating indoors every day, when the weather is good, try meditating outside; and in your meditation, try connecting with the nature spirits around you.

We talk about the importance of discipline, but you can practice discipline and still change your routine. A good activity to move around is number one on the first list: "Attending class and doing the class work beforehand." This can be done any time during a day or even the week.

Try mixing things up. Maybe read one day or evening and do the exercises another time. Keeping the same routine can become rigid.

Try adding an item or two from the second list to the first list. For example, you could incorporate the first item on the first list, "Having a daily routine of meditation," with number eighteen from the second list, "Developing your relationship with your Higher Self."

You could also take a minute during the day to connect to your Higher Self and ask it a question that is perhaps related to the work or activity you are doing. The more you work with it, the more you are developing it.

Sometimes it is good to take a break completely, other than from your routine of meditation. But even with that, you may try to meditate at a different time of day than you usually do. Maybe you need to do something in the morning and meditating would make it difficult to do. Instead of simply not meditating that day, try to find time later on to meditate for at least ten minutes. This is important so you keep the daily vibration strong.

If you are really overburdened with work, you may have to miss a class. Don't feel guilty about that—sometimes it happens. Just don't miss a series of classes because then you are starting another routine that is taking you away from growing spiritually. The same is true of doing the reading and the exercises. Buddy work should be done on a regular basis, but if you have to change the day or the time, feel you can do this if it is okay with your buddy. Again, with all of these things, if they become fanatical, then you are stopping your progress on the path.

The following story illustrates this point:

Larry had been a disciple for seven years. He had two initiations, which was a great achievement for that amount of time. He was single, twenty-eight, and actively dating. He worked as a financial consultant for a large investment firm. So far, his affairs had been short-lived, and he wasn't really interested in finding someone and settling down.

That all changed when he met Alexis at a party. It was love at first sight for both of them. She was twenty-nine, with a MBA in business, working for a large corporation as a manager in the product-development division. They were both professionals with a strong desire to grow professionally in their companies and a need to make a difference in their chosen careers.

From the beginning, Larry told Alexis about the teaching and how much it meant to him. She understood this and was accepting of his spiritual inclinations, even though the teaching wasn't something she was interested in for herself. Larry's teacher had always said a disciple didn't have to marry another disciple, or even someone interested in the teaching, as long as the partner didn't object to the disciple being in the teaching. Alexis was a good example of such a partner, as she had no objection and never minded when Larry went to class, meditated, and did his spiritual work.

All of this worked for a while, even after they decided to live together. Things started to change not because of Alexis, but because there were times when Larry wanted to do something with her, and not go to class. He got up early and always did his meditation—that wasn't a problem. But doing the classwork was hard for him to fit in. He would plan to do it after dinner, but Alexis would start watching a good film on TV, and when he went to get a drink he would stand and watch it a little and get hooked.

They also made plans with friends to go out to dinner etc. and some of those dates seem to interfere with his weekly buddy work. His buddy understood, but when it kept happening, she asked her teacher if she could have another buddy, as the work meant a lot to her. Larry was upset when she left him, and asked his teacher for another buddy, and promised to do better. With his new buddy he changed their meetings to every other week, not the weekly ones he had with his previous buddy. This worked out better for him, and his new buddy was okay with the arrangement.

Slowly all of Larry's routines started to come apart. His mediations were firm, but his attendance at class was less and less, as was his reading and exercise work. His teacher saw what was happening and asked him about it. Larry said he really didn't know. But he was very busy now that he was living with someone, and because of that, he just couldn't be as attentive to the teaching as he had been before.

He said to his teacher, "I thought it was all right to take breaks from the teaching once in a while." His teacher said, "Yes, but I said once in a while, not what you are now doing, which is all the time. I have always said the teaching should be a priority in your life. Also, that it should guide your life and your relationships. Instead, it is no longer a priority, and your relationship has taken that position. I don't think Alexis is asking you to do this, so what has happened to your personal striving?"

"No, she has been very good about my being in this teaching. She even asks me why I'm not going to class more."

"Then you need to talk more to your Higher Self and ask it why you are falling away."

Larry decided to go on a weekend retreat in a nearby Buddhist monastery. During that time, he worked with his Higher Self and discovered that his lower nature was using Alexis as an excuse to slowly leave the teaching.

He talked to his teacher about it and then told Alexis what was happening. She agreed, and said she had been concerned because it was clear to her, when she started dating him, that his spiritual needs were very important. She also said that if she could help him, she would be glad to. They looked at his schedule, and agreed they both wouldn't make social dates that included both of them on class days or buddy days. Larry would find time for the rest of his spiritual activities on his own. Also, Alexis decided to take some creative online writing courses that were of interest to her.

There are times when you need to look at your schedule and readjust it. Mixing it up makes the routine more interesting. One day you may decide to read the chapter for class and do the exercise. But then, something else comes up that you want to do. Never be fanatical. Don't stick to doing the reading and exercise because you feel you can't change your plan. Just see if there is another day and time you can do the work.

It's about being flexible, but it is also not about putting your study of the teaching off for something else that is not really important to you, just as an excuse to not do the work.

*Exercise One:*

*Look at the schedule you have made for the first five items that are necessary for you to do. If you don't have a certain schedule, ask your Higher Self the following questions:*

1. *Is it better for me to do these things in a flexible manner, or is it best to have a weekly schedule that I follow most of the time?*

2. *If the answer is that it is best for you to have a flexible schedule, then ask: Will I be able to fulfill all these things weekly?*
   - *If the answer is no, ask: Why not?*

3. *If the answer to the first question is that it is better for you to have a weekly schedule that you follow all the time, ask: Why?*

4. *Look at that answer and ask: Is there something I*

*can do to help me become more flexible?*

- *If the answer is yes, ask: What do I need to do?*
- *If the answer is no, ask: Why not?*

Sometimes, when someone wants to be more flexible, the person can't do it without causing her to wander off the path. Some people need to have things planned in a certain way in order to do the work. If you are one of these people, it is important to understand why. Do the following exercise.

*Exercise Two:*

*Ask your Higher Self the following questions:*

1. *Is this a pattern I learned in my childhood?*
   - *If the answer is yes, ask: Tell me what caused me to form this pattern?*
2. *Also ask: Is this something I brought over from a previous life?*
   - *If the answer is yes, ask: Can you tell me more about the life?*
3. *Is it possible for me to change this now and still get all the work done?*
   - *If the answer is no, ask: Why not?*
4. *Take that answer and ask: Can I change this*
   - *If the answer is yes, ask: Can you give me a first step*

*Exercise Three:*

*Reread the two lists at the beginning of this chapter. You now should understand the best way for you successfully to do the first five steps that are important for your spiri-*

*tual growth. Next look at the additional twenty items that would be good to include in your spiritual work. Separate out the ones that you never do on a separate list.*

*Look at each item on that list and put it in your heart and ask if this is something you need to try and do?*

*If you feel an item is something you should try to do, put it on a new, third list. Then take the this third list and ask your Higher Self the following questions for each item:*

1. *Why is it important for me to try to work on this?*
2. *Will I be able to fit it in my weekly schedule?*
   - *If the answer is no, ask: Is there any way I can fit this in sometime during the month?*
     - *If the answer is still no, ask: Then why did I get a positive reaction when I put it in my heart?*

Again, don't be rigid about doing everything. Balance your life and always try to enjoy what you are doing spiritually. If it just becomes something you make yourself do because you believe you have to, then the teaching will no longer be meaningful to you. It should always make you feel a sense of accomplishment, knowing that as you strive forward, it will bring you joy.

## Chapter Fifteen

# Seeking Wisdom

You may wonder why the title of this chapter is Seeking Wisdom, particularly if you are someone who is in the teaching or someone who is interested in the teaching, because then you would then be someone who is consciously seeking wisdom. *Wisdom* in this sense would mean the desire to grow spiritually; when someone has that desire and does go seeking, that person will eventually find wisdom. This of course is connected to striving for God Consciousness, which this teaching emphasizes.

When Wisdom is something that you desire, it is very different from the normal definition of it that relates to finding God Consciousness. Of course achieving God Consciousness will give you a certain kind of wisdom that relates to the spirit within you. This chapter is about a wisdom that is very different. It is not about discovering the Source and coming to a deeper understanding of higher knowledge. Instead, it is about discovering the wisdom within you. You may question how you can have wisdom within yourself when you are a neophyte, and even those who have been in this teaching for years may have the same question.

Working with the Higher Self is certainly part of discovering the wisdom within you. Yet there is another part of you that contains the wisdom that this chapter is addressing. This part is separate from the Source and even separate from the Higher Self, and it also belongs to both of those. That may sound incomprehensible. How can it be a part of the Source and the Higher Self and yet be separate? It can be both because it is wisdom that comes from having spent many lives evolving into who you now are. In those many lives you found wisdom through the experience of living, learning, and changing—bringing the knowledge only you have in your individuality. It belongs to no other person because only you went through those many lives paying off karma and accumulating karma to bring forward that knowledge within your consciousness. Your personal learning is your hidden wisdom, and only you can uncover and reveal it.

The wisdom in the Source relates to God Consciousness, which all humanity will someday relate to. The wisdom in your Higher Self is part of the Higher Mind, which can bring down the wisdom from the Source that belongs to all humanity. The wisdom within you that relates to your personal evolution is unique to your individuality. This is why everyone is a separate individual and no two people are the same—even if they are born together as twins.

As you strive in any spiritual teaching, there comes a time when it is important to be in touch with your personal wisdom, as it will help you on your spiritual journey.

The following is a list of those aspects in you that contain your wisdom:

1. Discernment
2. Intuition
3. The Heart
4. The Intellectual Mind
5. Striving
6. The Will
7. Creativity

*Discernment*—is the ability to know right from wrong. It gives you the innate understanding of what needs to happen in a given situation. It also helps you clarify knowledge that is given to you and determine what is correct or incorrect. When you meet someone, it helps you come to a better understanding of that person's character. Discernment works with the intuition to come to a deeper understanding of what is really happening. It takes many lifetimes of making and paying off karma to have a developed sense of discernment. Previously, spiritual teachings called it discrimination, but in today's world discrimination has taken on a meaning of racial, sexual, and cultural dislike and separatism. This is why the word has been changed to discernment.

*Intuition*—this refers to an inner knowing that is often abstract. It is also called one's "gut feeling." It refers to being in a situation that causes you to feel something isn't right or something is going to happen. Some people have a strong intuition, which again comes from many lives of developing self-awareness in dangerous or in other situations which can cause a person to face an outside conflict. It can also give you a feeling about someone you meet. Sometimes the feeling connects with your discernment to come to a better understanding that explains the feeling. For example, you meet someone for the first time and have an intuitive feeling that you have been with the person in a previous life. Your discernment may then come in to tell you that it was a good or bad connection.

*The Heart*—the chalice of the heart contains many accumulations from past lives. It holds the ability to love, to have compassion, to feel sympathy and empathy, and to experience inner peace. Most of all it contains the knowledge of right actions. A person with an open heart can mirror others and be someone who can help others realize what they need to do for themselves. A giving heart is just that. It gives to others in ways that go beyond physical and mental advice. Its energy is warm and healing. A heartfelt person has had many lives in spiritual practices that were full of devotion.

*The intellectual Mind*—is different from the Higher Mind, which is part of the Higher Self. This is the cognitive mind that is used in daily life. It contains the learning you have had in the present incarnation, but it also has within it knowledge that you have gained in past lives. Obviously, this knowledge isn't always something you may be using in the present life, but it sometimes can be accessed in a present situation. For example, if you were a leader in the past and had developed positive skills in doing that work, in this life, you may at some time need to take on a leadership role in a project you are doing. This could be something you haven't done before; but when you take on the role, you may find it is very natural for you to do. Hidden knowledge remains from life to life and can be rekindled. You may have been a classical musician in a previous life and never play an instrument in this life, but you immediately loved classical music, even as a child.

*Striving*—is a certain type of energy that comes through the heart. Some people have it naturally and use it in everything they do. In school, they study and strive for top grades. In their work, they try to grow and learn as much as they can. In a spiritual teaching, they strive to grow spiritually and follow the different practices that will help them in their process. These people always do well. It is not a matter of ambition, which comes from the ego; striving comes from many lives of devotion, discernment, and dedication. It is a positive energy that is very necessary in any spiritual practice. Without it, a person will lack the energy to confront psychological problems and follow his inner drive to grow spiritually.

*The Will*—This is probably one of the strongest components a person needs. Without a strong and skillful will, a person can't tackle and accomplish any given assignment—whether it is work or spiritually related. Will is essential to have if you are on a spiritual journey. It helps you face obstacles and challenges. It is also necessary for any mission or work assignment that you need to accomplish in life. Again, it is part of your accumulations from past lives. If you were a soldier, you needed will to go into battle; if you were a minister, you needed the will to guide your congregation; if you were a leader, you had to have it to direct others. In some of those lives you may have used the will wrongly and had to pay off karma as a consequence. As a result, you may not want to use it at all in fear of retribution. But in a spiritual teaching you need to use the skillful will in combination with striving. You need to use it with your heart to take right action, and you need to use it with your discernment and your intuition for right follow through

*Creativity*—Inspiration and creativity come through the heart. It is one of the most necessary energies that humans can have in all their lives. Without creativity, life is grey, dark, and lacking in hope. In the past, it was associated mainly with the arts and not recognized as a major component in all endeavors: whether in being a leader, working in an office, or being a lawyer, an accountant, or a scientist. No matter what the profession, even ones that seem based on factual work, the need for creativity is always there. It's the springboard to lift someone out of the mundane into realms that are full of invention. It contains beauty in its many aspects and is the source of the planet's evolution. Without it, a person lacks the essence of human life itself. Creativity is a source of joy.

All of above qualities are a part of your personal wisdom. They have existed in all your previous lives, sometimes completely, and many times almost imperceptibly, depending on your karma. It's important to seek your inner wisdom, bring it fully into your consciousness, and use it in your daily lives.

*Exercise One:*

*Taking each of the seven qualities, ask your Higher Self the following questions:*

1. *How much of this aspect do I use in my daily life?*
2. *Then ask, How much of this is stored in my chalice that comes from past lives?*
3. *If the amount is more than you are using, ask: Is there anything that is preventing me from using more of this quality?*
   - *If the answer is no, ask: How can I start to use more of what is contained in my chalice?*
   - *If the answer is yes, ask: What is preventing me from using more of this quality?*
4. *If the answer is that the amount in your chalice is less than you are now using, ask: Is it possible to continue developing this quality in this life?*
   - *If the answer is no, ask: Why not?*
   - *If the answer is yes, ask: Please give me a process and a first step to help me in continuing to develop more of this quality.*

Sometimes the chalice has less of a quality mainly because a person may not have had opportunities in some past lives to develop it. Usually people in this teaching have a background of living many lives, so it is rare when this happens. If your Higher Self tells you that you have less than 50 percent of a quality in your chalice, then it's important to have a better understanding of why this has happened.

If any of your seven qualities have such a percentage, do the following exercise:

*Exercise Two:*

*Ask your Higher Self the following questions:*

1. *Is there a reason I haven't developed this aspect over 50 percent in this life?*
   - *If the answer is yes, ask: What is the reason?*
2. *Then ask: Does this reason still exist for me in any way in this life?*
   - *If the answer is yes, ask: How can I overcome this so I can start to develop this quality more?*
3. *If the answer is no, there isn't a reason I haven't developed this quality, ask: Is it possible to develop it now in this life?*
   - *If the answer is yes, ask: Give me a process and a first step in developing it.*
   - *If the answer is no, ask: Why not?*

You may find that your chalice contains a great deal more than you are using. If for example, it contains 80 present and over of a quality and you are now only using 50 percent or less, then it would be good to explore this more.

*Exercise Three:*

*Look at your answer to the 3rd question above in which you ask your Higher Self: "Is there anything that is preventing me from using more of this?" Take the answer and ask your Higher Self the following questions:*

1. *Is the reason for this part of my childhood conditioning?*
   - *If the answer is yes, say: Please tell me what caused this and what is the best way for me to heal this?*

- *If the answer is no, ask: Did something happen in this life or a past life that caused this?*
2. *If the answer was that something happened in this life, say: Please tell me more about it and how can I heal it?*
3. *If the answer was that something happened in a past life, ask: Please tell me more about it and how can I heal it?*

When you do these exercises, you may find that the amount of a given quality in your chalice is the same amount you are using at this time in this life. It would be good then to decide what quality you would like to develop more. You can do this by consciously starting to work with the quality. Ask your Higher Self what is the best way to improve it and make it part of your daily life. Do a nightly review, and look back at the day, questioning whether you used the quality during that time. You needn't try to develop it only in your relationships with others, but you can also watch your thinking and feeling. Are you bringing this wisdom in your thoughts? Are you experiencing this wisdom in your feelings and heart?

Realize that you can develop each and every one of these seven aspects—discernment, intuition, heart, intellectual mind, striving, will, and creativity—and in that development you will grow spiritually.

### Chapter Sixteen
## The Importance of Being Disidentified

When someone starts to work in a spiritual teaching, it is important to understand some of the main goals to strive for. One of these is the ability to disidentify when you are in an emotional situation.

*Disidentify* is a word that is often not fully understood. It differs from not being involved or passive and even from not being concerned. Someone who can disidentify is someone who is fully involved in what is happening, but is able to step back from it and see clearly what needs to be done. This is because the person has the ability to completely let go of any emotion, and stay centered, and observant. Only then can the person know intuitively what the next step needs to be.

This is true not just in a situation that involves others, but it is also true when a person feels overwhelmed with personal inner feelings, and is trying to know how to handle and heal those feelings. Being stuck in the feelings keeps a person from truly understanding them, but stepping back and seeing them with an open heart gives the person the ability to go deeper in that understanding. This is what is meant by disidentifying.

When a person has been able to disidentify, then he can truly know the best way to achieve wholeness and inner peace. The following is a story that illustrates this:

Gerry was a student in Higher Self Yoga and was studying with one of the teachers. He was consciously striving and hoping to become a disciple. During this time, he was dating Prisha, a woman who was more advanced and a disciple of a different teacher in Higher Self Yoga. Gerry was happy to be with her as he truly felt she could help him to learn more about the teaching, and also how to open his heart to his teacher.

He was an intellectual and had a PhD in physics, working as a professor at one of the local universities. Because of this, he believed the mind was a better instrument than the heart, and even though his teacher told him he needed to work more with his heart, Gerry found it too difficult to do.

He lacked devotion, which was one of the reasons he hadn't become a disciple.

When he talked to Prisha about this, her advice was to simply try using his heart in small ways. For example, Gerry had a dog and Prisha told him to cuddle his dog and feel the love in his heart for him. He told her he always did this—that loving his dog, or friends, or even her was easy for him to do. She was surprised when he included her name and asked him directly if it was true that he loved her.

He said, "Yes, I do love you. You are a beautiful person, but I'm not madly in love with you in a romantic way. We just started dating so I'm not sure if that will happen." Prisha replied, "But you can love someone with your heart, and even though it isn't in a romantic or madly in love way, the person can still feel the love when it is being sent. I'm saying this because I don't feel your love for me at all, because it's not coming from your heart."

"But if it comes from my heart in such a way, it has to be romantic."

"No, that's not true. If your love is not emotional, which

romantic love usually is, then it can still be strong because it is disidentified."

Prisha tried to explain to Gerry what being disidentified meant, but it was too hard for him to understand. Gerry went to his teacher and told her what Prisha said and his teacher replied, "Yes, she is right. If you are disidentified from your emotions, you can feel unconditional love for someone or even a group of people, and that feeling has no attachments but is pure love that comes from your heart to others."

"Why would I want to do that? Why would I want to love everyone?"

"Unconditional love opens your heart and helps you feel joy in everything you do or see. It opens you to all possibilities. It brings you focus on all things around you, such as beauty in nature, in art, in music. It brings you compassion and understanding.

"Unconditional love contains devotion, which you lack because you are always in your mind. It's not about personally loving everyone. It is about experiencing the true essence or spirit in each person, and in that experience understanding that person and being there if the person needs you."

His teacher then added, "Being in your emotions without being disidentified stops you from having this; it keeps you centered on your ego self, your needs, and your desires. Learning to disidentify is an important part of this teaching and a goal that everyone striving to grow spiritually needs to learn."

Gerry asked her, "How can I start to learn how to disidentify?"

She replied, "Ask your Higher Self to help you and ask it to give you a first step."

Gerry tried doing this and began to become disidentified in small ways. If he got upset with something, he stepped back, and tried to let it go, and experience it from a place of observation. It was a long process, but he stuck to it and eventually started to feel what it meant to be disidentified. Slowly, the process helped him work with his heart, and he realized that he could use the heart in combination with his mind in his work and his relationships, including his relationship with Prisha.

In order to be disidentified, you need to understand those areas in your life that can cause you to be emotional. The following are some of them:

1. Romantic relationships
2. Marriage
3. Difficult mundane situations
4. Family intrigue
5. Raising children
6. Authoritarian people
7. Illness
8. Competition
9. Challenges and obstacles
10. Facing life-threatening situations

*Exercise One:*

*Look at the list above and determine if any of these circumstances are part of your life. Write down each one that you feel can cause you to become emotional, including an overview of what happens and why you become emotional.*

*After you have made this list, think about anything else in your life that you know can cause you to be emotional. Add that to your list. Next prioritize the list, putting the circumstance that makes you feel the least emotional on top. The last area on the list will be the one that makes you the most emotional.*

*Taking the first area, ask your Higher Self the following questions:*

1.  *What is the best way for me to handle this situation and be more disidentified when I am in it?*
2.  *Take that answer and ask: Is there anything that will stop me from doing this?*
    *   *If the answer is yes, ask: What is it, and how can I prevent this from happening?*
3.  *Try to remember a scene in which a situation made you become emotional. Play that scene over again in your mind. Imagine you are above looking down on it. Next following the Higher Self's advice, see yourself replaying the scene. Notice how you are feeling when you do this. Are you less emotional? If so, notice if there are others in the scene, and how they are reacting to your new way of responding*

Work with the situations on your list slowly. It's good to start with the ones that don't affect you the most so that you can develop the ability to be disidentified.

As you practice this process, be aware that each time such a situation occurs in your life, you can make a choice of falling into your emotions and responding in the way you have always responded, or you can step back, realize what is happening, and practice becoming disidentified.

Obviously, the situations at the bottom of your list are the ones that will be the most difficult to change. Work with those only after you have practiced the less difficult ones, so that you will have developed the skills to tackle them.

While you are doing this work, something may come up that again causes you to become emotional. Be kind to yourself; you can't change overnight. Give yourself credit when you can become disidentified even for a short time.

This chapter has mainly been emphasizing personal emotions because they are the major cause to prevent someone from disidentifying. But there are also other situations that can keep you from being in a disidentified place. They are:

1. You are overwhelmed with work
2. Someone you love needs special care that only you can provide
3. Your children need more discipline
4. You have an active role in your community
5. The politics in your country have become negative
6. You are looking at the future and what you will be doing
7. You see others who need help

These are all things that can be time consuming and cause you to be mentally involved so it is difficult to try to be disidentified.

*Exercise Two:*
*Look at the above list, and if any of them relate to you, write them down in detail. Also, think about your life. Is there anything that is time consuming (even if it's not emotional) that you would like to be disidentified from. Take your final list and ask your Higher Self the following questions about each item:*
  *1. How can I best be disidentified when I am in this situation??*
  *2. Take that answer and ask, Is there anything stopping me from doing this?*
    *• If the answer is yes, take that answer and ask: How can I prevent this from happening?*
Sometimes it takes more than just the desire to be disidentified;

you also need the ability to stop during the chaos, center yourself, and go inward to find your place of calm. Only there can you come to where you can be disidentified. This ability is one you can learn and practice, as it will help you in all aspects of your life. It is what is commonly called *mindfulness*. When you can practice mindfulness it will help you to find your core and use it in all the above areas that this chapter has touched on.

Your Higher Self is the key to helping you do this practice. It knows you and understands those areas in your life where you can become overwhelmed and lose you sense of purpose. The following exercise is to reconnect you to your Higher Self and practice disidentification with its help.

*Exercise Three:*

*Link with your Higher Self and ask it the following questions:*

1. *Can you please help me understand what aspects in my life will take me away from being connected to you?*

2. *For each aspect, ask the Higher Self: Please tell me what I need to do to overcome this obstacle.*

3. *Take that answer and ask: Is there anything that will stop me from doing this?*

   - *If the answer is yes, take that answer and ask: How can I prevent this from happening?*

*When you have finished these three questions, again take each thing the Higher Self has given you and ask:*

1. *When this comes up in my life, how can I remember to stay disidentified?*

2. *Take that answer and ask: Is there anything stopping me from remembering?.*

- *If the answer is yes, ask: what is it, and how can I prevent this from happening?*

In all the work you have been doing in this book, try to reflect back to those areas and situations that keep you from being in your Higher Self. Realize that being disidentified is being in the Higher Self. It is a quality of the Higher Self that is prevalent in all the work. The more you learn to practice disidentification the easier it will be for you to connect to your Higher Self. The Higher Self is practical as well as spiritual. It can help you in your daily life, it can show you the way to overcome some of your psychological problems and of course, it can guide you spiritually. Keep its qualities alive within you by practicing disidentification.

### Chapter Seventeen

# Challenges that Can Stop You on the Journey

When you start a spiritual journey, there are many factors that you need to examine and confront. They can be personal beliefs as well as beliefs that come from your family conditioning. Often the family keeps these beliefs in order to continue the tradition moving onward from generation to generation. Some of these are based on the culture you grew up in, and some are based on what you were told by your parents and grandparents. For example, a person's family heritage might be Italian. Her parents and grandparents always married within the Italian tradition, mainly because they lived their lives in Italy. Only when they came to the United States did that tradition go through some changes. On the other hand, sometimes that Italian tradition is so strong that the American family still marries other Italians living in their neighborhoods. Then all the cultural background is steadfastly kept. When a person from such a background marries someone who is not Italian, it can produce conflict in the family, usually with the older generation.

This dynamic can also hold true when it comes to someone who studies a spiritual teaching that is not related to that person's background. For example, if someone is raised in a certain religion and decides to pursue a different one, the family may be very upset and try to change the person's mind. It can particularly become a problem if the religion is a strict one that the whole family is involved in. For example, if a man, who comes from an orthodox Jewish background, decides to leave the religion, his family may disown him. It could even be worst if he marries a Christian woman, who won't convert to the Jewish faith.

The same thing can happen if someone from a strict religious background decides to pursue a spiritual teaching such as Higher Self Yoga. It can also be a problem if one person in a marriage decides to study Higher Self Yoga and the person's partner objects and feels threatened. Any exoteric or esoteric teaching that is part of the yoga system can seem very foreign to a spouse who believes in a traditional religion.

To pursue a spiritual teaching takes time and dedication, which can also make a spouse feel resentful. When there are children involved, this can cause more conflict if the student wants the children to understand the teaching. The following is a story that illustrates this situation:

Francesca, an Italian American, was married to Antonio, also Italian. They had both grown up in the same Italian neighborhood in New York City.

They married in their early twenties and had their children right away— Maria was now age twelve, Isabel was ten, and Joseph was eight. After the third child was born, Francesca broke from the family tradition and used birth control pills, even though Antonio objected. They both came from families with eight children.

Settled in a house on Long Island, Francesca was an accountant and was able to do much of her work from home, and Antonio was a manager in a corporation.

The family were all good Catholics, attending Mass every Sunday. Antonio even taught one of the Sunday School classes afterward, which the children went to.

Francesca's best friend, Madeline, also was a Catholic, but she was not as devoted as Francesca and her family. One day at lunch, Madeline told Francesca she had discovered a spiritual teaching that she felt was her right path. It was called Higher Self Yoga. They talked for long time about it, and during the conversation Francesca felt her heart fill with a spreading warmth—a feeling she had never experienced before. She asked Madeline if she could go to one of her classes. The following Tuesday evening, Francesca attended the class and immediately knew that this was her true calling, and that the person who was leading it, Alex, was her spiritual guide.

After attending several classes, she asked Alex to be her teacher. He accepted her but told her she needed to be honest with her husband and tell him about her decision. Francesca protested, "He would be very angry about me doing this and leaving the church. He thinks I spend my Tuesday evenings with some friends in a knitting group."

"That's why it is important to tell him the truth. You don't have to stop going to church—you simply have to explain that there is a spiritual teaching that you are studying, and Jesus is also part of this teaching. Tell him it is Higher Self Yoga and yoga means union with God."

"What if he still objects? I'm sure in his mind yoga is something strange and eccentric and should not be taken up unless it is the physical yoga exercise."

The following Sunday after dinner, while the children were playing outside, Francesca spoke with Antonio. Following Alex's advice, she prudently told her husband about the teaching. His reaction right away was one of disbelief and anger that she was doing something like this behind his back.

Francesca explained what had happened, and that she felt this teaching was a continuation of her spiritual journey. She would never leave the church, but wanted to study a teaching whose goal was to achieve God Consciousness. She stayed in her heart and spoke carefully, with love in her voice, clarifying that she understood why Antonio could feel this was wrong for her to do, but she knew it was her spiritual path and her destiny.

Unfortunately, Antonio couldn't listen, but instead became even angrier and forbade her to attend the classes anymore. He felt it sounded like a cult and was shocked by her lack of discernment. He implored her to go to confession and talk to their priest.

During this time, Francesca kept linking with Alex, she realized it was best to not continue the talk until Antonio calmed down. She explained this to him and went out for a walk. On the walk, she called Alex and told him what had happened.

Alex said, "Yes, I was there and know how difficult this was for you to do. You did the right thing by not continuing to talk to Antonio while he was so upset. When you return, tell him that you love him, but that he needs to understand this is your spiritual teaching and that you aren't going to argue with him about it."

Alex added, "If he can't accept this, then it might be good to go to a marriage counselor to try to heal this discord."

When she returned, Francesca calmly again spoke to Antonio and suggested they should seek help to resolve this conflict. He refused and became obnoxious, saying that the group had brainwashed her.

Francesca resolutely continued to attend class. When Antonio protested, she told him that if he tried to stop her, she would leave him. Finally, when Antonio realized that Francesca would not listen to him, he agreed for them to go to a therapist.

During therapy it became apparent that Antonio felt he should be in total control of Francesca and the children. Francesca had experienced this attitude at times before but hadn't really seen to what extent it existed—mainly, because she loved him and was busy with her work and raising the children. She also realized that in her Italian heritage men were accepted as being dominant and in charge. It was an important awakening to her that her life was being ruled without her permission.

Unfortunately, Antonio was too embedded in his beliefs to try to change, and in the end, Francesca separated from him and eventually divorced him without his consent. Her family was also unaccepting of her actions. It was a difficult decision to make, but she knew it was the right one for her. She realized it was also important for her daughters not to be brought up in a tradition that was ruled by the men of the family.

Francesca continued on her spiritual path and became a disciple of Alex. Her love for the teaching kept her centered and independent in life.

Francesca's story was an extreme one. Even though she wanted understanding from her family, their background was so strong and grounded in traditional beliefs that she was not heard. Her independence wasn't accepted by most of her family, including her parents. Only a few relatives realized it was all right for Francesca to live a life that was based on her own beliefs. Fortunately, two of her sisters stay connected to her and in their own way have also tried to break from some of the family traditions.

*Exercise One:*

*If your family in any way objects—or if you feel they would object—were you to enter a spiritual teaching, ask your Higher Self the following questions:*

    *1.  What do you believe the main objection would be?*

    *2.  Is this objection something that can be resolved?*

- *If the answer is probably not, ask, Why not?*
  - *Take that answer and ask, Tell me how best to handle this situation so that it can be resolved.*
    - *Again, take that answer and ask: After I do this, and it still isn't resolved, what is my next step?*
    - *Also ask: If it is never resolved, what is the best way for me to continue on the path?*

Another deterrence that can happen when a person starts her spiritual journey is having feelings of being overwhelmed. These feelings come up when someone who is new realizes that the path will take a long time to travel. She may feel that a lot of her personal time will be needed to succeed and grow in the teaching, which would limit her enjoyment of the pleasures that exist around her.

Also, in the Higher Self Yoga teaching a student is meant to do service in the world. Service can open a student's heart, especially if it involves doing something in the community that will help others. It can be anything that takes you into areas where people need assistance, whether it is helping the elderly, or sick, or simply working in food kitchens, or donating food to those in need.

The following is a list of things that a student is expected to do.

1. Attend classes
2. Meditate
3. Work with a buddy who is also in the teaching
4. Attend yearly retreats
5. Study the books
6. Do service

All of these are important to do, but often a person has too much mundane work and too many things to accomplish that prevent her from following through with the spiritual work. Higher Self Yoga is not a strict teaching. It is understood that there are many distractions in life that keep a person too busy to do the above six activities.

There will be students, though, who give up the things they enjoy in order to do all the spiritual work. These students can become fanatical, which is a trait that will stop spiritual growth.

There are also students who put the teaching at the bottom of the list of things to follow through with. These students are the opposite of those who are fanatical. They lack the enthusiasm and the desire that a person needs to move forward on the path.

The teaching needs to be balanced in your life—it should not be so time consuming that you don't do anything else other than your mundane job; nor should it take a back seat to all the other activities that fill your daily life.

*Exercise Two:*

*Look at your spiritual practice. If you think you may be doing too much spiritual work, ask your Higher Self the following questions:*

1. *Am I doing too much spiritual work and not allowing myself to enjoy other activities?*
   - *If the answer is yes, ask: What is the best way for me to become more balanced in my everyday life?*
     - *Take that answer and ask: Is there anything preventing me from doing this?*
     - *Take that answer and ask: How can I change this?*

- *Take that answer and ask: Is there anything that will stop me from doing this?*

*If you are fanatical in your striving in a spiritual teaching, the main thing to realize is that there can be some past conditioning that is causing this. Ask the Higher Self the following questions:*

2. *Did anything happen in my childhood conditioning that made me fanatical?*
   - *If the answer is yes, ask: What happened to cause this? Take that answer and ask: Is there anything preventing me from becoming more balanced?*
3. *Then ask: Do I have a past life in which I was fanatical?*
   - *If the answer is yes, say: Please tell me about it.*

Sometimes if your childhood conditioning had no discipline and direction, you may just not know how to focus more on the teaching. You may also lack commitment to the teaching and the teacher. If you had a fanatical spiritual life in the past, it could cause you to lack commitment now in fear that if you truly devoted yourself more to the teaching, you would become fanatical again.

In a past life you could also have suffered some injustice in a spiritual teaching or even in your vocation that causes you unconsciously to be afraid that it could happen again now.

This last chapter of the book is about finding balance in your life. In so doing, realize that balance gives you a sense of joy that your life can be full both spiritually and in everything else you do. A spiritual teaching should never be a burden or something you feel you need to do. It should give you a sense of wholeness, which is the basis of who you can truly be.

# Higher Self Exercises

## The Mountain Exercise

Sit down in a comfortable chair.

Close your eyes and feel your whole body relaxing. First your feet are going to relax, then your legs, your thighs, your stomach, chest, shoulders and arms, your neck, and head. Now your whole body is feeling relaxed.

Take some deep breaths and center yourself by linking with your heart chakra, which is located in the center of your chest.

With each breath feel the cares of the day dissolving into nothing and try to let go of any thoughts and feelings.

Now imagine you are standing in a meadow and right in front of you is a mountain. You are going to climb the mountain, and it will be a very easy climb and at the very top you will meet your Higher Self.

For now, you start to walk on the path, which is in front of you. Almost immediately you enter a forest. It's a forest of tall evergreen trees and pine. You can smell the pine and as you walk on the path upward you can feel the pine needles under your feet.

You can hear the birds singing and the rustle of leaves in the woods.

And as you slowly climb upward there are rays of sunlight breaking through the branches lighting your way.

Now you are leaving the forest and you continue climbing upward on the path. There are trees and rocks and grass and as you climb you can feel the warmth of the sun on your shoulders. It's a beautiful summer day, with a gentle breeze blowing. You continue to climb upward.

Suddenly, you hear the sound of a waterfall. You leave the path and go over to the side of the cliff and look up toward the top of the mountain and see a beautiful waterfall cascading down. As the water hits the rocks nearest you, feel the wet spray on your face and hear the roar of the water as it hits the rocks beneath you.

You turn now and go back to the path and continue climbing upward. Now there are no more trees, just big boulders of rock, and scrub brush and sand. You stop for a minute and see that there are other mountain ranges on either side. You can look down and see the meadow from where you came.

You turn and continue climbing upward. Now you are coming to the top of the mountain and as you go around a bend you see at the very top a flat plateau of land and on the plateau is a bench. Sit down on the bench and take a moment to look around you. Experience the beautiful view of mountains all around you.

As you sit there feel the warmth of the sun on top of your head. Now look up at the sun, which is directly above you. As you look a figure is going to appear and slide down on a sunbeam and stand in front of you. The figure is your Higher Self. You may also experience It as a light or a feeling of warmth and expansion in your heart chakra. When you feel you are experiencing It, imagine the sun shining down on It and notice if It changes. If It stays the same or gets brighter then It is your Higher Self. If it disappears or gets dark, tell it to leave and try the exercise again.

Imagine reaching out and holding the hands of your Higher Self, linking your heart to Its heart. Feel Its energy flowing to you. How does that feel?

When you feel connected ask the Higher Self your questions.

Listen to Its answer, which may take the form of actual words, thoughts, or impressions.

As a check for the information you've received, ask the Higher Self for signals of verification, or if there have been no direct answers, ask for signals in answer to your questions, for example, a signal for a yes answer, a no answer, a maybe answer.

When you feel ready to end the conversation, thank your Higher Self, open your eyes and write down everything that has occurred.

## The Meadow Exercise

Sit down in a comfortable chair.

Close your eyes and feel your whole body relaxing. First your feet are going to relax, then your legs, your thighs, your stomach, chest, shoulders and arms, your neck and head. Now your whole body is feeling relaxed.

Take some deep breaths and center yourself by linking with your heart chakra, which is located in the center of your chest.

With each breath feel the cares of the day dissolving into nothing and try to let go of any thoughts and feelings.

Now imagine yourself standing in the middle of a meadow. It is a beautiful summer day, the sun is shining brightly and there is a soft breeze blowing.

Experience the meadow around you — the trees, the green grass with wild flowers growing, and the mountains in the distance.

You can smell the sweetness of the air and feel the warmth of the sun and the gentleness of the breeze.

You may want to take your shoes off and feel the grass under your feet.

In the distance, across the meadow a figure appears and slowly walks toward you. You know the figure is your Higher Self. As It comes closer try to sense what It looks like. Is It a man or a woman? Is It just a light or do you simply sense it in some way? The Higher Self will come to a stop in front of you.

When you feel you are experiencing It, imagine the sun shining down on It and notice if It changes. If It stays the same or gets brighter, then It is your Higher Self. If it disappears or gets dark, tell it to leave and try the exercise again.

Imagine reaching out and holding the hands of your Higher Self, linking your heart to Its heart. Feel Its energy flowing to you. How does that feel?

When you feel connected ask the Higher Self your question or questions.

Listen to Its answer, which may take the form of actual words, thoughts, or impressions.

As a check for the information you've received, ask the Higher Self for signals of verification. If there have been no direct answers, ask for signals in answer to your questions.

When you feel ready to end the conversation, thank your Higher Self, open your eyes, and write down everything that has occurred.

*(The above two exercises are adapted material from the book* Psychosynthesis, *by Roberto Assagioli.)*

### The Garden Exercise

This exercise takes you into a garden. Imagine you are entering a walled garden. The entrance way has a trellis of climbing roses over it. As you enter you see two paths. One on the left continues to follow beds of roses. The one on the right has a variety of flowers arranged by color. Some beds are golden, full of lilies and smaller orange and yellow flowers. There are also beds of blue and purple hyacinth and Iris. Put your favorite flowers in the beds. This path continues down to where there is a small, paved circle of stone with a bench on it. You sit down on the bench. Your Higher Self is coming down the opposite path and stands in front of you. Continue the exercise by first shining light on It.

If you choose to walk down the path of rose beds you will see all varieties and color of roses. This path also comes to a round paved circle of stones with the bench on it, and you also see the Higher Self coming down the opposite path to stand in front of you. When you feel connected ask the Higher Self your question or questions. Listen to Its answer, which may take the form of actual words, thoughts, or impressions.

As a check for the information you've received, ask the Higher Self for signals of verification. If there have been no direct answers, ask for signals in answer to your questions.

When you feel ready to end the conversation, thank your Higher Self, open your eyes and write down everything that has occurred.

## The Lake Exercise

This exercise is for the water lovers in the group. Imagine you are in a boat on a beautiful lake. You are rowing or paddling toward an island. You pull up to the island and dock your boat.

You get out of the boat and walk down a path that takes you to a paved pavilion that overlooks the lake. There is a bench; you sit wait for the Higher Self. You see It is in a boat on the lake. It comes to a dock in front of you and gets out and meets you on the pavilion.

Then shine light and continue the exercise.

When you feel connected ask the Higher Self your question or questions. Listen to Its answer, which may take the form of actual words, thoughts, or impressions.

As a check for the information you've received, ask the Higher Self for signals of verification. If there have been no direct answers, ask for signals in answer to your questions.

## The House Exercise

In this exercise you imagine you are sitting in your home meditating. The doorbell rings and you go to the door and open it. On the other side is your Higher Self. It enters and sits down across from you.

Shine light and continue the exercise.

When you feel connected ask the Higher Self your question or questions.

Listen to its answer, which may take the form of actual words, thoughts, or impressions.

As a check for the information you've received, ask the Higher Self for signals of verification. If there have been no direct answers, ask for signals in answer to your questions.

When you feel ready to end the conversation, thank your Higher Self, open your eyes and write down everything that has occurred.

I suggest you try each exercise on different days and choose the one, which gives you the best results. Use the exercise that you feel works best for you to get in touch with the Higher Self.

*Disclaimer: All exercises, suggestions and information provided are for general information purposes only, do not constitute professional advice and are not intended to substitute for the guidance of a professional or specialist. All use is therefore at the user's sole risk and responsibility. The author and Higher Self Yoga Inc. assume no liability or responsibility whatsoever for any loss or damage of any kind regardless how arising.*